£1·25

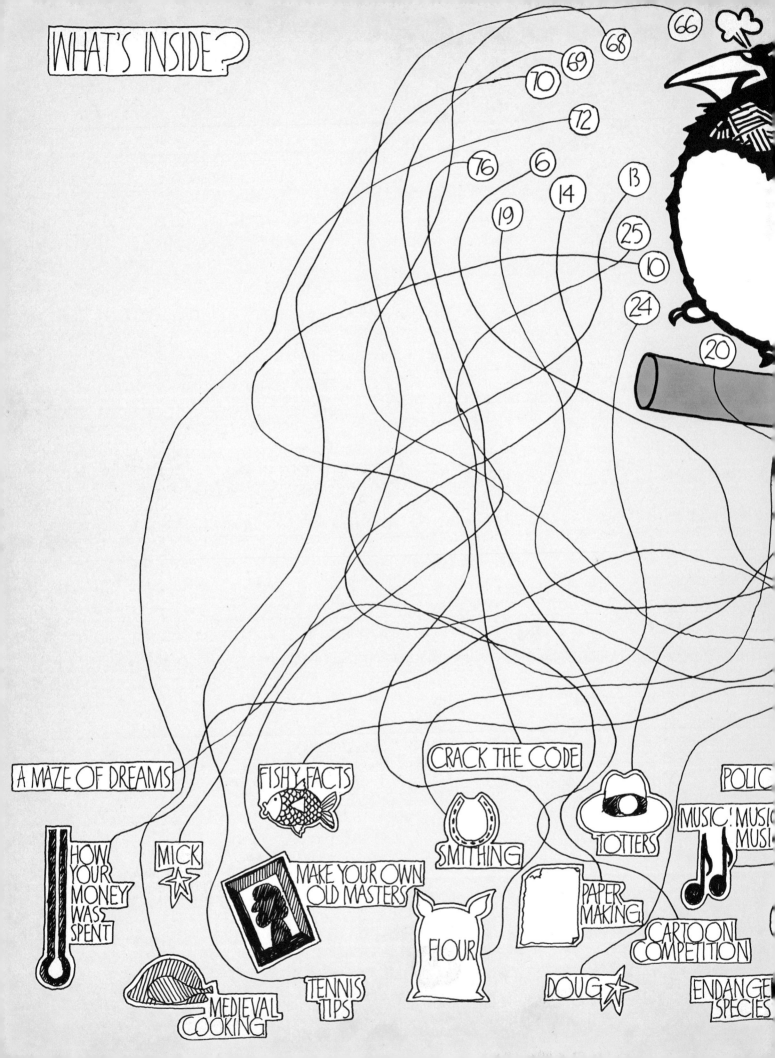

Music! Music! Music!

Hands up all those who don't like music!

Well of course no one is going to put their hand up to that, because we all like music in one way or another, whether it be rock, reggae or Rachmaninov! And that goes for Mick, Doug and Jenny. Mick, a budding pop star himself, is rather partial to rock and is quite an authority on up and coming groups. Doug on the other hand goes for jazz, and the big band sound, and he even has a drum kit at home so he can play along with his favourite records. Jenny freely admits to being a great singer – 'my voice grates and grates' – but she does hope to become the world's very first triangle and tambourine superstar; she likes any sort of music so long as it has a melody that you can sing in the bath!

Over the last year Magpie has tried to reflect some of the many faces of music, from the funky soul of chart-topping group Ace, to the classical expertise of

Paco de Lucia, one of the world's greatest flamenco guitarists. One group that provoked a lot of interest was F.B.I. who made their very first TV appearance on Magpie. When this funky soul band came on the show they told Mick that they were so new that they had neither a manager or a recording contract. Mick mentioned this fact on the programme, and before long the switchboard was jammed with people trying to sign them up! It took over three hours to sort all the enquiries. Look out Hughie Green, opportunity knocks on Magpie as well! Another TV first came for Flame, one of the youngest pop groups ever to appear on the programme. The average age of the band was only 15, and their lead singer and bass player, Mike Wilson, was just 12 years old. In fact his guitar was nearly as big as he was!

Judging by your letters a lot of you play the guitar, so we tried to show as many different types of guitar music on Magpie as possible. Representing American blues music, the type originated by Negro slaves on the cotton plantations of the American deep south over 100 years ago, we had Stephen Grossman, a young guitarist from New York. He was virtually a one man band, playing the bass notes with his thumb, the melody on the top strings with his little finger, and scratching out a rhythm accompaniment with any other fingers that he had left! Nearly 400 of you wrote in to find out just how he managed to do it.

Another popular guitar item was provided by Pete Willsher, one of the top steel guitar players in this country. The steel guitar, or Hawaiian guitar as it is often called, is rather like a normal guitar but with the strings standing well away from the fingerboard. To play the instrument you use a piece of steel tube that is slid up and down the strings, producing a strange singing sound. Pete told us that it all started in Hawaii in 1895 when a Hawaiian bone carver found an old guitar that had been left out in the sun. The neck was so warped that he was unable to play it in the normal way, so he tried sliding a piece of bone along the strings. He soon became very popular with his strange guitar and the weird music that he made, and lots of his friends started copying him. Now the Hawaiian guitar is as much a part of the culture of the Islands as the hula dance, and Steve McGarrett and the boys of Five-O.

Last but not least we had Paco de Lucia, a guitar genius if ever there was one. Paco comes from Andalucia in Southern Spain, and is famous for his fiery Flamenco music, the music of the Spanish gypsies. Paco started playing as soon as he was old enough to hold a guitar, and now he is one of the most highly respected players in the whole of Spain. His fingers move in a blur as he plays, and in certain passages he can cram nearly 80 separate notes into one second! His secret? Practise, practise and practise again.

But it isn't just guitar music that we've featured on Magpie, for we have also had visits from Richard Harvey, who came into the Magpie studio to show

Mick, Doug and Jenny his collection of medieval recorders, ranging from the tiny Garkleinflotlien to the huge Bass recorder. He told Doug that the word 'recorder' comes from the Italian 'ricardo', which means present or keepsake, because in olden days people gave each other recorders as little gifts.

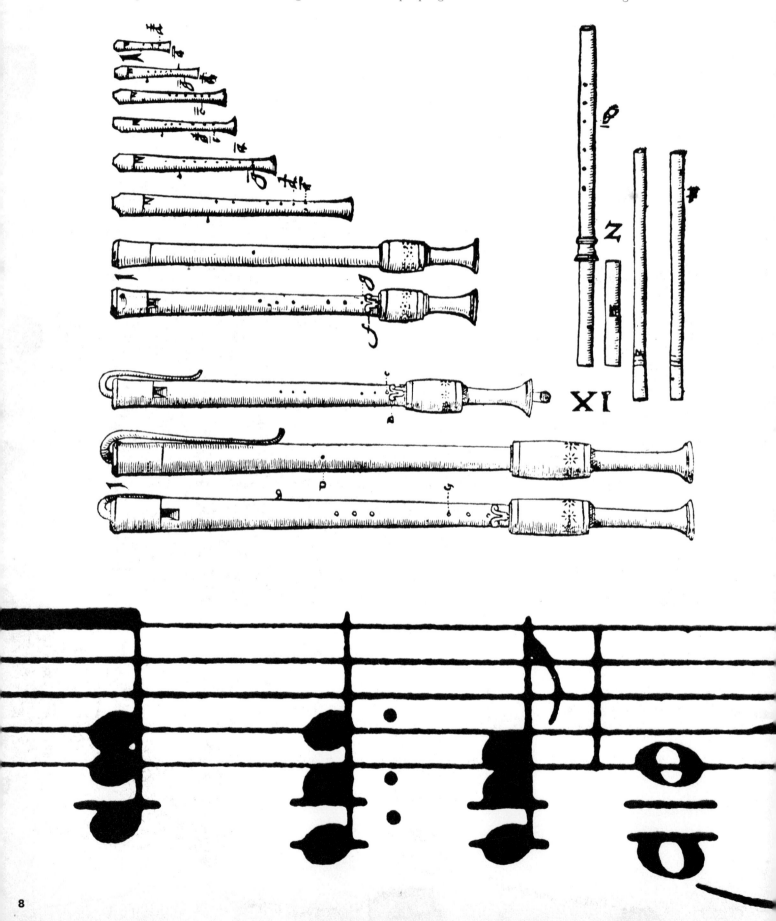

Another visitor was Japanese percussionist Stomu Yamashta, who demonstrated the noble art of percussion, or hitting things to make music. The first piece that he played was on conventional drums and cymbals, then he amazed everyone by playing a kitchen! Lined up in the studio was an assortment of frying pans, saucepans, fish slicers, a kitchen clock that rang on cue – everything save the proverbial kitchen sink. And then Stomu moved in like the Galloping Gourmet, hitting everything in sight, and out of a collection of cutlery came music, each pan giving a different note as it was struck. Jenny said afterwards that Stomu proved that you can cook and make music at the same time.

Another unusual instrument featured on Magpie was Muff Murfet's jug. Muff plays with a folk quartet called Jugular Vein, who proudly boast that they have been turned down by every recording company in the country. As well as the usual folk instruments like banjoes, guitars and double bass, Jugular Vein make music on empty jugs and bottles. Muff showed Jenny that if you make a 'razz' noise into the neck of an empty flagon, bottle or jug, you can get a nice deep booming sound. In fact in days of old many jazz bands which could not afford a proper double bass would use a large jug to make bass notes. When Jenny tried, all she got was a red face! Perhaps she didn't puff enuf!

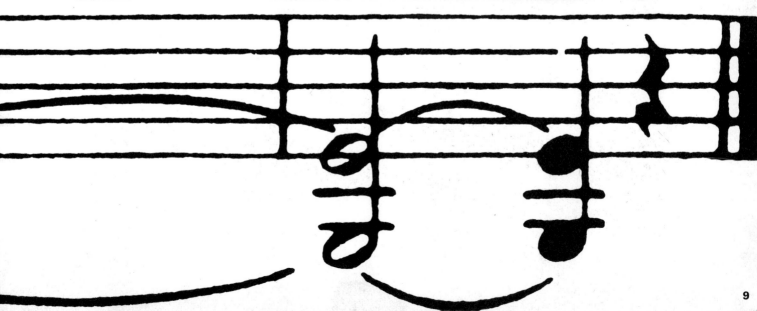

FLOUR

How many times a day do you eat food that contains flour? Even if you're someone who tries not to eat cakes and pastries, flans and pies, the chances are that you eat flour at least once a day in a slice of bread. Flour is one of the 'staples' of the British diet. It is made from wheat, which you saw being grown and harvested on Mr Threadgold's farm. Last year Mick thought he would follow that wheat and see how it is made into the flour that you buy in the supermarket. So off he went to Holme Mills where Jordan's flour is made.

Wheat and barley have been milled at Holme Mill on the River Ivel, for nearly 900 years. It was first mentioned in the Domesday Book when, together with its sister mill, it was valued at the princely sum of 47 shillings as part of the estate of Ralph de Lisle. The mill remained in the hands of great landowners until 1611 when it was bought by Edward Ferrers and Francis Philips. Under these two worthy millers it flourished as an independent mill in the heart of England's corn-growing area.

It is now owned by the Jordan family. When they first took it over, more than 100 years ago, Holme Mill was only one of 400 mills in Bedfordshire. Today it is the sole remaining privately owned mill in the county. In 1896 William Jordan modernised the mill, replacing the old millstones with roller mills, and since then it has remained largely unchanged. Its main source of power is still the water wheel, and the six-foot fall of river water ensures a steady 25 horse power to power the rollers and other machinery.

Mick got to the mill just as huge lorries were arriving with sackfuls of grain. Before milling can begin, the grain must be cleaned. So it is hoisted to the top floor of the mill. Here it is sifted and all the stones and weeds that have got into it during harvesting are riddled out. (Some batches of grain have been known to give up pen-knives and other such unlikely objects.)

The grain then goes into huge hoppers where the moisture content is regulated. It ought to be 15 per cent. If it is too dry, water is added, and sometimes it needs drying.

Now the milling can begin. Milling is really the process in which grain is ground between a series of steel rollers. The first set of rollers are grooved. They move at different speeds in order to break up the grain. The grain is cracked and the white 'semolina' is scraped off the husk.

The semolina is then elevated to the floor above and sieved. The pure semolina then proceeds to the next set of rollers while any that is still impure goes back to be scraped again.

Grain is sometimes rolled and sifted as many as seventeen times before it is finally reduced to flour.

The last sets of rollers are smooth, and it is at this stage that the wheat germ is flattened and sieved out, leaving white flour.

The miller keeps a close eye on the milling process and adjusts the rollers by the 'Miller's Thumb' principle. By rubbing the flour between his left forefinger and thumb he can tell whether the rollers are going too fast and heating the semolina, or whether they are too tight. If the flour feels slightly sharp, the rollers must be adjusted or else the baking quality of the flour will be affected.

The final sieve is made of silk mesh. Mick watched the flour pass through the silk and heard the miller, Bert Goodson, pronounce his satisfaction.

One last process before the flour goes to the packing department: because the wheat germ has been taken out, the law says that synthetic vitamins and calcium must be added to replace what has been extracted from the white flour.

Holme Mills produce 60 tons of white flour and 35 tons of brown (or wholemeal) flour every week. However, Bill Jordan, a member of the fifth generation of Jordans running Holme Mills, told Mick that brown flour is becoming more and more popular and over the last five years they have been producing more of it. Wholemeal used to be the traditional flour of poorer people, and in Victorian times it became more fashionable to eat white flour. The trend is now back to brown flour in which all the goodness and vitamins in the wheat are retained, whereas they are taken out of white flour and replaced by chemicals.

The flour is packed by machine into 3-pound bags for the supermarket. An extra $1\frac{1}{2}$ ounces of flour is put into each bag to make up for loss of moisture during travelling and storing. The machines can pack thirty-six bags a minute.

When Mick returned to the Magpie studio from his enjoyable day at Holme Mills, he tried baking a loaf. He wasn't too successful—though it was not the flour's fault—but see if you can do better with this recipe, which uses both white and wholemeal flour:

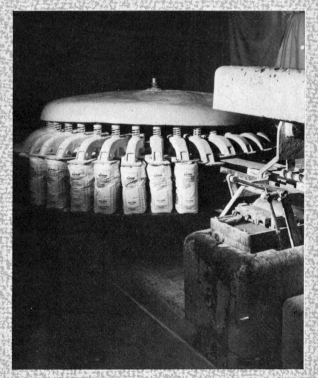

IRISH LOAF

$\frac{1}{2}$ lb plain flour
1 tablespoon baking powder
1 teaspoon bicarbonate of soda
A pinch of salt
$1\frac{1}{2}$ lb wholemeal flour
1 tablespoon caster sugar
1 oz butter
$\frac{3}{4}$ pint warm milk

1 greased baking sheet.

Sift together the plain flour, baking powder, bicarbonate of soda and salt into a bowl and mix in the wholemeal flour and the sugar.
Rub the butter into the dry ingredients in the bowl until the mixture looks like fine breadcrumbs.
Pour in the warm milk and stir until the mixture forms a stiff, smooth dough.
Shape it into an oblong loaf, score across the top and bake at 400°F (Gas Mark 6) for 1 hour until the loaf has risen and turned golden brown.

Paper-Making

Most paper is made from wood. To make a ton of paper, as many as fifteen trees have to be chopped down and used. Imagine all the things that are made of paper and you may get an inkling of how many trees are being destroyed.

Paper can be made from waste-paper – old newspapers for instance – and even from other waste materials such as old clothes, rags, carpeting and nettles. Real paper mills can cost up to 50 million pounds. But here is a method, used since 100 BC in China, and shown on Magpie by Colin Cohen, for making paper in your own kitchen (Mum allowing)!

You need:

1 food blender, 1 mould (a wooden frame covered with a tightly stretched nylon mesh), about 10" x 8", 1 basin large enough for the mould to be dipped into, lots of old newspapers or other waste paper (the more the merrier), some pieces of felt each about 11" x 9", 1 mangle (optional), 1 piece of hardboard (optional), 12" x 10"

This is what you do:

Tear up the paper into small pieces and loosely fill the blender. Fill it up with water and blend until the mixture is a pulpy mush. Turn it out into a basin, fill that up with more water and stir, until the mixture is a little thicker than milk. Dip the mould into the basin and lift it out with the mush on the surface.

Allow to drain, then turn it over onto a piece of felt. (It is better if the felt is damp.) Lift mould off carefully and cover the mush with another piece. If you have difficulty getting the paper mush off the mould and onto the felt you can make one sheet at a time and dry it on the mould. Do this a few times making a 'sandwich' of layers of felt.

If you have a mangle you can put the 'sandwich' on a piece of hardboard and squeeze it through the mangle. Then hang the felts up to dry. (If you have no mangle just separate the sandwich, and hang each layer up to dry, but the felt will drip a lot.)

When dry, carefully peel the paper away from the felt so you are left with a sheet of paper. If you want a smoother surface you can iron the paper when it is dry.

If you don't get a good piece of paper the first time try again, perhaps changing the quantities of paper or water you use. You're bound to make a lot of mess, so cover the floor with newspapers. For more info: Making Paper (Practical Science Projects) Ginn & Company, Aylesbury. Price 30 pence.

Fun-Art Farm

by Wendy Buonaventura

Kentish Town is in one of the most heavily populated boroughs in London. The area is being redeveloped at the moment, and whole streets are being torn down. Wander around the area and you'll see many houses boarded up waiting to be demolished, and lots of busy building sites. It is not the sort of place where you would imagine finding anything to remind you of the countryside.

Yet wait a minute. In one of those shabby rows, between two tall houses, there is an opening. Above the opening a gaily painted sign reads

A farm? In the middle of London? Walk down the opening and through a gate at the bottom and you will indeed find yourself in the entrance to a farm, with animals roaming all around. There is an indoor riding school (the only one in London not owned by the Queen) and a collection of animals that includes a cow, goats and sheep. These animals wander freely around the barnyard while ducks, rabbits, chickens and guinea pigs are netted-in for safety.

What is the story behind the farm? Who would think of such an idea? And why build it right in the middle of a big city?

The idea was thought up by Ed Berman of Inter-Action (a Kentish Town group working with local people). As for the last question—a notice on the farm gate provides a clue to the answer:

As you know, there is not much chance if you live in a city of coming into contact with animals, apart from behind the bars of a zoo. Three years ago Inter-Action started exploring ways of setting up a farm. Their aim was to give kids in Kentish Town a chance of becoming involved with animals and learning how to take care of them. The opportunity came when they were given permission to use three acres of waste land owned jointly by the local council and British Rail.

The land had originally been used for stables which housed shunting ponies that worked on the railway further along. In the cottages next door lived railwaymen who looked after the ponies. But many of these cottages had been standing empty since as far back as 1890 before Inter-Action came along. You see, once animals were no longer used on the railway there was no need to keep them nearby. So the land became a timber yard and in time simply fell into disuse.

With the help of local people Inter-Action set about a huge transformation task. Rubbish was cleared, the old cottages repaired and a covered-in riding area set up in what had been the timber store. Materials for rebuilding and kitting-out the farm were donated by neighbouring firms—even today the ponies get their bedding free from a nearby timber merchant. Meanwhile, fathers of kids in the area gave up their evenings to help repair the riding-school roof.

With all the voluntary help given it took only two months to complete the main part of the work. To complete the entire farm cost £5,700 altogether. This may sound a huge amount of money, but it's about fifteen times less than it would cost to build an ordinary playground with swings and a football pitch.

Now, two and a half years later, the farm is a hive of activity. It is Kentish Town kids who use it most, though anyone may visit. But

PLEASE TOUCH AND FEED THE ANIMALS PROPERLY

SEE EILEEN

admission to the area is on the understanding that you help with the work. It requires an enormous amount of work to keep the farm on its feet. Therefore everyone who uses it must take some responsibility for its running. So on arrival you go and ask for a job to do (those who know the ropes will always teach those who don't).

One of the first things you notice when walking around is how gay everything is. The inside walls of the stables are bright with country scenes painted by the kids during the summer. A ceiling-high mural designed by one of them extends all the way around the walls: animals beneath a rainbow in big bold colours, surrounded on every inch of wall by flowers and trees. Outside in the barnyard a hump-backed serpent with red and yellow markings all down its back lies in the path of unwary visitors; though having lurked in the same spot for a few years now it's a little the worse for wear. Further up there is a group of life-size animals made out of concrete with scrap-wire innards. These were made by a member of Inter-Action, helped by the kids, and include a pony on which you can practise mounting.

The tack room has become the farm's general meeting place, and people will call there to meet friends even if they are not having riding lessons on that particular day. In one corner they have been assembling what looks like a miniature museum. Pinned to the wall are copies of old maps showing what Kentish Town looked like in bygone days. Even more intriguing, there is a glass cabinet housing a treasure of Victorian bric-à-brac. Each item was dug up a few yards away and is labelled with the name of the finder. There are tiny stone jars, carved clay bowls for pipes and old apothecary bottles made out of coloured glass. You may have seen some of these coloured bottles before. In Victorian times glass containers were not sterilised and used again as, for example, milk bottles are now; instead they were simply buried at the bottom of the garden. Who knows what curious bits and pieces are still lying under the soil of the Fun-Art Farm? (Or under that of any garden—perhaps your own.)

At one end of the farm on land owned by British Rail stand a series of allotments. These are worked by Kentish Town people, who often supply greens for the Fun-Art rabbits. And then there is a gardening club for the elderly.

As you can see, a nice mingling goes on between people of all ages down on the farm.

Kids will help the old people carry water and manure up to their allotments; in exchange some of the old men have fascinating tales to tell about the work that horses were made to do in days gone by.

Finally we come to the picnic area—a circular patch closed in by trees and shrubbery. Of course, it is not much used in cold weather, though it has been the scene of many a camp fire and Guy Fawkes party. But when the weather turns warm you will see families laden with baskets of food trooping up there on Sunday afternoons.

Kids of all ages often visit the farm with teachers from their school. They get a chance to feed and handle the animals, and may finish their stay with an acting session up on the picnic area.

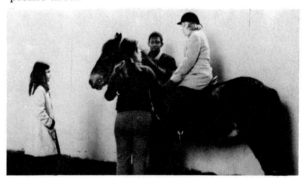

Riding—at ten pence a session—is for five-year-olds upwards. Kids who are mentally or physically handicapped come at weekends, while those from nearby have their turn during the week.

Half the lesson is spent learning how to look after the ponies: grooming, feeding, watering them and mucking out their boxes. Because the farm is in the city it means there is no real grazing land to be had, apart from that in the picnic area. So on Sunday afternoon regular Kentish Town riders take the ponies to graze on Hampstead Heath, a couple of miles away.

It is quite a sight to see Fury, the Shetland pony, jogging along with the others. He has a special saddle—a pink one with sequins and an ostrich-plume headdress. The kids made this finery for him one Christmas; they would dress him up as a kind of Santa Horse and take him around Old Age Pensioners' parties to swell the festivities.

If the ponies have been out on a long ride and are tired they are given bran mash by way of a treat. This is made in the same way as porridge, using bran instead of oats. The bran is mixed with boiling water and salt, then covered until it has cooled down a little. It is good for helping relax the animals, who work very hard. As you can imagine, the riding school is one of the most popular activities and unfortunately there has to be a waiting list.

Everyone using the farm takes part in running it. Those who work on the allotments have their own rules, while the stables too have a committee. In this way everyone has a say in what goes on. For example, if the kids feel any one of them is disrupting the activities, they have to work out what to do with that person. The worst thing perhaps would be to ban him or her from using the farm; yet so far this has not happened to anyone.

This then is the story of the Fun-Art Farm. Inter-Action set it up for two reasons: firstly as a place for the people of Kentish Town; secondly to show what you can do if you have a little money, some waste land and a lot of goodwill from people.

But what of the future? The redevelopment plans mentioned at the beginning are going to affect the farm. Already, on the other side of the road, men are at work on a new housing estate. Eventually houses and a road are destined to run right through where the riding school and animal pens now stand. Of course everyone agrees that housing is needed here more than a farm. Many people think it is unreasonable to expect an indoor riding school in the middle of London, anyway. But some have pointed out that a riding school—in this area where there are few open spaces for people to go and enjoy themselves—is no more a luxury than, say, a park. The point is that none of these are luxuries. All are necessary to people. It is no good having a new house to live in if you haven't got anywhere you can go and let off steam occasionally.

Shortly after the Fun-Art farm opened it was discovered that a dustcart depot had been planned for the site. The kids were determined to try and keep the farm. Twenty of them, aged between ten and seventeen, formed the 'Save Our Farm Junior Action Group' to drum up support from people in the area. They printed 'Save Our Farm' on badges and T-shirts and made a video film explaining why they thought it was so essential to Kentish Town. One lad said simply: 'If it closes down there will be nothing for us to do anymore.' They spent the summer enlisting help from adults then presented a petition to the Council. It was signed by nearly 2,000 people—some from

outside the borough—and was the first petition in the country organised by kids themselves. In the end the Council agreed the dustcart depot could go elsewhere.

Yet there is a big difference between finding a new site for a dustcart depot and finding one for a road and houses. So it looks as though whatever becomes of the farm it will have to move elsewhere. We are hoping, at least, that British Rail may let Inter-Action put the riding school on the waste land beyond the allotments.

Some of you may be interested to know that British Rail, local councils and other public agencies are among the biggest landowners in the country, and quite a bit of their land is not being used at present. Usually it is little patches of wilderness just waiting for people to come along with good ideas for it. This may mean that if, for example, a group of people decide they want to set up their own City Farm, land could be made available for it. But it would only be borrowed. In the end, when it could no longer be spared, it would be returned to its owners.

It would not be easy to set up a farm. You would have to gain the support of many people— parents and teachers and perhaps someone on your local council. The main problem, of course, would be money. The Fun-Art Farm supports itself by hiring out some of their riding lessons to local authorities. Nevertheless, it is quite expensive to keep even such a small project going. Setting up allotments would be much easier, as there is less money involved.

Inter-Action runs a service which gives free advice to outside groups. It has already received hundreds of letters from people asking how they too can get permission to use plots of vacant land. So who knows? Perhaps before long we will be seeing City Farms dotted all over the country. We'll just have to wait and see.

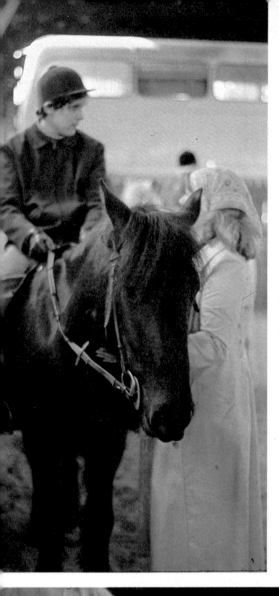

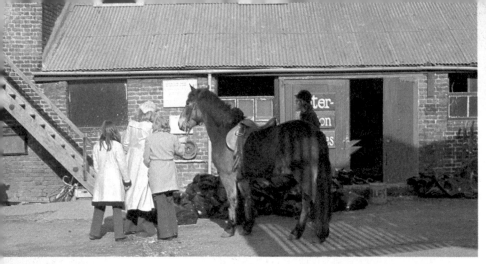

Fashion Flash

If you're fed up with your old clothes but can't afford to buy any new ones at the moment, transform the rags into glad ones! Change the length of your garments, for instance, by chopping off the bottoms of some things and adding them to others.

Take a full-length skirt and a full-length smock, say. Cut the bottoms off each and trim both with lace. Add the bit of smock to the bottom of the skirt and you've got the layered look, with a smock to match!

Brighten up any old trousers or jackets, or even skirts and shirts, with patches of quilt. Decorate pockets with rick-rack braid. Add sequins for a glittering effect!

I SHALL BE GLAD TO GET TO LONDON IF ONLY TO GET THESE BOOTS OFF!

1977 is Jubilee Year – twenty-five years since Queen Elizabeth II came to the throne.

EARN A MAGPIE BADGE

These are the Magpie Badges. You could own ten of them. Each one means that you have done something special. So why not see how many you can collect? This is what you have to do to get each badge.

The Original Magpie Badge
This badge is only given for an especially good letter or drawing or anything which has taken much more time and trouble than usual to complete. You cannot ask for this badge.

One for Sorrow
If you have spent one night or more in hospital, let Magpie know, and ask your nurse or doctor or your parents to sign the letter.

Two for Joy
When you have passed any sort of test or examination, write Magpie a letter and ask your teacher to sign it.

Three for a Girl and Four for a Boy
These badges are given to girls or boys who write an interesting letter to Magpie on any subject they choose. A good drawing or painting can also qualify for these badges.

Five for Silver
This is a very special badge. You are given it if you send in a really original idea for a Magpie programme item. Write in detail about how you think the item should be arranged for the programme, and if Magpie likes the idea, you will have earned the badge.

Six for Gold
All you have to do to qualify for this badge is send Magpie a tall story, preferably of your own invention.

Seven for a Secret Never to be Told
If you think that one of your friends has done a good deed, write and tell Magpie, giving your friend's name and address, and they will be sent the badge. You cannot nominate yourself, but if you have done a good deed you can always qualify for the badge by asking a friend to write about the deed to Magpie.

Eight for a Wish
All runners-up in Magpie competitions receive this badge.

Nine for a Kiss
Jenny gives this badge to any boy or girl who has learnt to swim since 1 July 1970. Your letter should be signed by your parent or guardian. *Mick* gives it to anyone who writes to him about a visit to an interesting place, such as a museum, historical building, art gallery, etc. Tell him what you liked best about your visit, and what you learned from it. *Doug* gives this badge to anyone who takes up a sport they have never done before, or who introduced a friend to a new sport.

Ten for a Bird You Must Not Miss
You can only be awarded this badge if you actually appear on Magpie.

GRAND PRIX

Last year Mick and Doug went up to the British Grand Prix at Silverstone. They got there early in the day so that they could follow the build-up to the big race. In particular, they wanted to follow the fortunes of a British driver with a promising future, James Hunt of the Hesketh team. Mick met him as he arrived by helicopter in the middle of the Silverstone track. He'd had a busy morning signing books and autographs at the Hesketh caravan and then doing radio interviews. Finally it was time to change into his fireproof long-coms and all the rest of his racing gear inside the old Hesketh caravan. Then he joined his mechanics in the pits to have a last check over that very important car, No. 24. Meanwhile, Doug had a look at the Ferrari van that carries cars like No. 12 of Niki Lauda who was leading in the world championships at that time. Some people thought that Tom Pryce from North Wales would be the next world champion – here he is with his Shadow car. Doug also saw Emerson Fittipaldi, the current world champion, and had a look at some other cars : the John Player Special, Clay Regazzoni's flame red Ferrari and Emerson's brother Wilson Fittipaldi had his car there. The only lady in the race was Lella Lombardi. A few minutes before the start, the clerk of the course gave a briefing to the drivers. James Hunt asked about the new starting system which was by light instead of the traditional flag but the drivers were assured that the lights wouldn't fuse. Tension mounted among mechanics and spectators. Cars were pushed onto the grid. . . . James Hunt relaxed in his car . . . Last minute instructions were given. One-minute siren – deafening noise – they were off – off on the British Grand Prix – 67 laps, 196 miles. At the start, the lead changed hands about 6 times and James Hunt was in the lead for 7 laps. Just then the heavens opened and down it poured. 12 cars went spinning off the track and the race had to be stopped on the 55th lap ; this meant that Emerson Fittipaldi from Brazil was the winner and James Hunt finished 4th. He did very well and, who knows, perhaps a British driver will be the next world champion.

Make Your Own Old Masters

Well, they don't have to be old masters. You can mount any picture in this way and make it look good. You may have a print of your favourite pop star or football player that you think needs special treatment. Or a picture from an old calendar, Christmas card or magazine could be used. (Don't try mounting pictures from colour supplements, though, because you'll find the print shows through from the back of the picture.)

As well as your picture, you need:
A piece of wood about 1 inch thick, which is the same size or a fraction smaller than your picture.
Black poster paint, a paintbrush, glue, a pair of scissors, a cloth, an old saucer, clear varnish or lacquer, wood dye (a natural shade like 'oak' looks best), a hook, white spirit or turps for cleaning the paintbrush.

Paint black all over the wood except for the side on which you will stick your picture.

Spread glue all over the unpainted side, especially on the corners.

Carefully stick the picture on the wood. Working from the centre, use a cloth to press out any air bubbles. Trim off any overlapping edges of the picture, using scissors.

Put a small amount of wood dye in a saucer. Dip a paintbrush in the varnish and then in the wood dye, and rapidly brush all over the picture. You will get a streaky effect which gives the picture that 'old master' look. The more you brush the less streaky it will be. Leave to dry completely, then put a hook on the back and hang it up in your room.

The painting on the right has been mounted by the 'Old Master' method.

The two 'Old Masters' above are (left) 'Market Cart' by Thomas Gainsborough & (right) 'The Chair and the Pipe' by Van Gogh.

ROUND LONDON MARATHON

The race started one Saturday morning at 9.00. My Captain, Nick Cripps, and I found we had to compete against 55 other teams. All sorts—ladies' teams, the armed forces and even some youngsters.

Nick had just won the Speedboat Personality of the Year award, but that wasn't going to help, as it was really a matter of timing. So, after getting the boat ready, we had to check the maps, the mileage and the rules with Len Britwell, one of the officials . . .

Then, when all was ready, Robin Knox-Johnson waved the flag and, at 15-second intervals, we were off.

. . . before synchronising watches.

Down the Thames at precisely 6 miles per hour, past the Houses of Parliament, under Tower Bridge to the first great obstacle.

A 20-foot wall at Limehouse.

Last year, Jenny bravely agreed to take part in this annual race, in which teams of two people take an inflatable dinghy, an outboard engine and a quantity of petrol, and race from Putney Bridge, along the Grand Union Canal, then back along the Thames to Putney Bridge again. Jenny tells the story of her adventure:

A quick cup of soup and off to Little Venice, arriving . . .

. . . just before we sank.

We also had three more breakdowns and nine locks which we had to carry the boat around, before checking in at City Road, Islington.

Unfortunately, the engine had been waterlogged and we lost precious moments changing plugs.

I got up the ladder first with the rope, closely followed by Nick, then the agony of pulling up both boat and engine began. It seemed impossible but, at last, we got it over the edge and safe.

A few seconds to get our breath back, and then on again.

Next day, having mended the boat we staggered to the start.

The Hanwell flight is seven locks, one after the other. We set off African style, the front of the boat on my head . . .

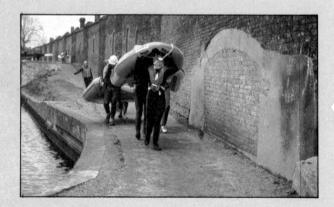

. . . with the engine cutting into Nick's shoulder at the back. We didn't stop once, I'm proud to say—though if we had, I doubt if I'd have got the boat back up again.

A very cold morning and about three hours of doing nothing but keeping to the clock. We were under constant secret watch.

This signpost meant more agony.

There were still *more* locks, believe it or not, before we hit the Thames again at Brentford.

... and thanking Nick for helping me through the last two days ...

Finally, we made it to Putney and, after lifting the boat out for the last time ...

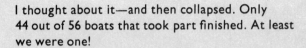
I thought about it—and then collapsed. Only 44 out of 56 boats that took part finished. At least we were one!

How I loved the Thames at that moment!

But, there was also another 20-foot wall, and as if that wasn't enough ...

... the tide was out, so we had to pick up the boat and wade into deeper water.

29

Smithing

Look at a blacksmith's anvil and you can somehow guess from its primitive shape that it belongs to an ancient trade. Yet it is a trade which thrives today, as Douglas discovered when he visited Mac, a Buckinghamshire blacksmith.

Mac and his two apprentices are constantly kept busy. As well as working at the forge, he has a van full of portable equipment with which he can shoe horses at studs and on race-courses. And he has to be ready day and night in case a vet calls him to take off the shoe of a horse in pain.

Doug had to be reassured that it doesn't hurt a horse at all to have its shoes yanked off and nailed on. Hooves, Mac explained, are like our finger- or toe-nails – they have no feeling at all. And like our nails, hooves keep growing. That's why horses need their hooves trimmed and their shoes renewed as often as every six weeks.

Race-horses are given specially light shoes, made of aluminium. Hunters are sometimes given special shoes with studs, to help them grip the mud. And special shoes can be forged to make horses walk properly, or to stop them slipping.

The shoes that Doug saw being made, though, were for ordinary horses and ponies. They are made of iron which Mac buys in long strips. He must measure each horse's hooves so that he can forge the metal into made-to-measure pairs.

Before he gets to work with hammer and anvil, he cleans the horse's feet, yanks off the old shoes, then clips away the surplus growth from the hooves. Then, the measurements complete, he cuts off the correct length of iron.

The iron is then heated, so that it is soft enough to be hammered to the right shape. Heating is done in the forge itself, which is fitted with electric bellows and burns coke. (In the old days the bellows were worked by hand and Mac showed Doug one of these.) The sulphurous smell of the coke is characteristic of blacksmiths' forges. The red-hot iron is then hammered into shape on the anvil.

Now Mac 'burns on' the shoe. This is the final fitting stage, when the hot shoe is put on the hoof and an indentation is made. Douglas was anxious again that this might hurt the horse, for puffs of smoke came from the hooves as Mac burned on the shoes. Mac promised it didn't hurt at all – and certainly the pony seemed quite placid about the whole procedure.

The necessary adjustments made, the shoe is then 'set' in cold water before being nailed into place. All blacksmiths' nails are made in Sweden and are quite expensive. Each nail is driven at a different angle through the dead tip of the hoof. Four nails go into the outside of the hoof and three into the inside. Then the nails are 'clenched up' – twisted off with a claw hammer to leave just a small tip, which is hammered flat and rasped smooth.

A brush-around with linseed oil to keep the hoof in good condition, and the pony is newly shod.

To become a blacksmith, you have to serve a four-year apprenticeship, spending up to eight weeks a year at a recognised college. After an apprentice has served a trial period of six months, he receives a grant from the Worshipful Company of Farriers, which is the body that assesses his exams at the end of the apprenticeship.

For the first two years, an apprentice blacksmith does simple tasks such as cleaning the horses' feet, removing the shoes, clenching-up and tending the forge. Gradually, the apprentice starts working on his own, and when he's passed his exams he usually sets up his own forge as a qualified and highly skilled craftsman.

Smithy Quiz

1. What is another name for the tune called 'Greensleeves'?
2. Who is the patron saint of farriers?
3. What is the proper name for an apprentice blacksmith who has served four years?
4. What is the proper name for a blacksmith who has served two years as a qualified smith?
5. Which composer wrote 'The Harmonious Blacksmith'?
6. What is the origin of the superstition that horseshoes are lucky?
7. Who wrote this verse and in which poem does it come?
   What the hammer? What the chain?
   In what furnace was thy brain?
   What the anvil? What dread grasp
   Dare its deadly terrors clasp?

HOUSE OF GLASS

C. M. Gleason

Kevin Brown and his sister Millie climbed out of the taxi and sighed in unison as they surveyed the frontage of number 68 Hollydene Avenue. It was a tall, Victorian terraced house in a large north-eastern town.

'Doesn't look much of a place to spend a holiday,' grumbled Millie, as their mother paid the taxi-driver.

'It might be fun inside,' said Kevin, without much conviction.

'Come on, you two. It's only for a week,' said Mrs Brown encouragingly. 'I'll be picking you up next Saturday.'

'A whole week,' said Millie dismally, as she lugged her case to the doorstep.

'Now then,' said her mother quite sharply. 'Northumberland's very interesting and historical. There's Hadrian's Wall, and . . . all sorts of Roman places and things,' she finished vaguely. 'You'll be able to write essays about them when you go back to school.'

'Whoopee,' murmured Kevin, and Millie giggled. Unfortunately, Mrs Brown heard.

'You must remember we're lucky to have a holiday at all this summer with Daddy working away so much,' she said, ringing the doorbell. 'It's very good of Aunt Natalie to put you up, or rather put up with you, until we can go and join Daddy in Scotland.'

'I bet Aunt Natalie is about seventy and smells of lavender,' whispered Millie.

The door was opened by Aunt Natalie herself. She was about seventy and smelled of lavender.

'Welcome! Janet, my dear!' cried the old lady, embracing their mother. 'And the dear children. Come inside, please.' Her voice carried strong traces of her original Russian tongue. She led them into the old-fashioned drawing room, a slim, fragile little person with lively blue eyes and snowy hair piled into a neat chignon.

'It will be so good to have children in the house for a while – but I suppose I must not call you "children", having grown so tall!'

'Well, Kevin's nearly thirteen and Millicent's eleven now, Natalie,' laughed Mrs Brown. 'So they – is anything wrong?'

Aunt Natalie had stopped short and was gazing earnestly at Millie.

'No . . . that is . . . Janet, who does Millicent most resemble?'

'Ah, I thought you'd notice that,' said Mrs Brown. 'She's very like Helena, isn't she?'

'To the life,' said Aunt Natalie. Tears dimmed her eyes and there was a look of mingled pleasure and sorrow on her lined face.

The door opened and a plump, bustling woman came in. She was introduced to Millie and Kevin simply as Anna, Natalie Veronik's companion. Anna had also been born in Russia, but thirty years of living in England had muted her accent so that it was barely noticeable. She was good-natured and friendly, and about twenty years younger than their Aunt, who explained that Anna would be taking them out in the car to the seaside and places of interest during their stay. Millie and Kevin felt much brighter as they followed her upstairs to their rooms on the second floor to unpack.

'Perhaps it's not going to be as dull here as we thought,' said Kevin, and Millie agreed.

After a cheerful dinner Mrs Brown had to leave to catch the train home.

'Mummy,' whispered Millie as they kissed her goodbye, 'who's Helena?'

'Sssh.' Their mother waved to Aunt Natalie and Anna, and led them out of earshot towards the taxi. 'Helena Veronik was your Aunt's daughter. She died young, and very tragically. You look very like her, Millie. Now, behave yourselves both of you and have a lovely holiday. Anna's really a lot of fun and she'll look after you very well. Oh, and Millie, try not to mention your ballet lessons. Helena was a dancer, you see?'

Mrs Brown climbed into the taxi and waved as it whisked her away. Back inside the house, Millie and Kevin had a conference with Aunt Natalie and Anna. They decided on a trip to the country with a picnic lunch if the weather held the following day, to see the Wall and the site of a Roman camp which was being excavated. Before long they were yawning, tired out with their long journey, and Aunt Natalie suggested bed, which sounded a very good idea.

In his room, Kevin was annoyed to find his watch broken. He had left it on the bedside table after having a wash before dinner, and the glass had cracked across its face. He was wondering whether he had knocked or dropped it during the journey, when there was a knock at his door.

'Look at this mess, Kevin.' Millie dumped her small vanity case on his bed. The mirror on its lid had shattered, and slivers of glass glittered among the contents of the case.

'You must have bashed it on the train,' said Kevin, helping her to pick out the pieces of glass. 'Hey, you've brought your ballet shoes along. I thought your teacher said you weren't to practise on your own at this stage?'

'Oh, a few *pliés* won't do any harm,' said Millie, frowning as she picked bits of glass out of the case. 'Mind your fingers, these pieces are very sharp. There, that's the lot. Thanks, Kevin. D'you think it's going to rain tomorrow?'

Kevin drew back his curtains and they peered anxiously out. The moon was riding serenely high in the clear night sky. Kevin turned to Millie with a grin. 'Not a chance,' he said.

Sure enough, the next day dawned bright and beautiful. Aunt Natalie fussed happily over the picnic basket as they all piled into the car. They were all in a holiday mood as they headed for the country.

'Oh look!' cried Millie in astonishment as a sheep leapt from the grass verge and over a low hedge at their approach. 'I didn't know sheep could jump!'

'Townie,' teased Anna. 'They are quite agile, the sheep,' their Aunt told them.

Natalie Veronik was their mother's half-sister. Her father was a Russian who had moved with his family to Poland after the Russian Revolution. Natalie had married Serge Veronik, who had been killed, along with her mother, when the Nazis invaded Poland. She had managed to escape to England with her father and her little daughter Helena, and of course Anna. At first they settled in London, where her father had married again. He died shortly after Millie's and Kevin's mother had been born, so of course the children had never known their grandfather. Natalie decided to live in Northumberland; she had never re-married.

All this the children gathered, in a rather sketchy way, from questioning their Aunt as they drove along. She seemed quite pleased with their interest, and promised to tell them stories of her hair-raising escape from Poland through occupied Europe, thirty years ago.

They picnicked near the ancient Wall in the mild September sunshine. Probably because it was late in the year, there were no other tourists about, and the only thing that slightly marred their day was the return of Millie's hay fever, which had troubled her during the hot summer months. She tried not to make a fuss about it, but was secretly rather glad to be away from the fields and back in the car that evening.

There was no television at 68 Hollydene Avenue. While Aunt Natalie was resting in her room and Anna was cooking supper, Kevin yawned and said, 'I wonder what the attic rooms are like in this house? We haven't been up to the third floor yet.'

'We can go and see if you – atishoo! 'Scuse me – like,' said Millie.

They went out on to the landing, tiptoeing past their Aunt's room so as not to wake her. There was no light bulb for the top floor, and the white attic door at the top of the stairs gleamed pale and rather sinister through the evening gloom. For some reason he could not name, Kevin felt an odd reluctance to climb further.

'Achoo!' sneezed Millie behind him. 'This wretched hay fever. Go on, Kevin.'

Slowly he mounted another couple of steps.

'Millie! Kevin! What are you doing?' They froze in shock at their Aunt's furious shout.

'Come down at once!'

Sheepishly they turned back down the stairs. Their Aunt was looking flushed, angry and somehow taller when they confronted her on the landing.

'We were just . . . just going to have a look at the attic, Aunt Natalie,' stammered Millie.

'There is nothing of interest up there. You must avoid that part of the house, *especially after dark*.'

Was it imagination, or was there a trace of fear in her voice?

'Come to supper now, I am sure it must be ready.' She turned and stalked downstairs.

Kevin shrugged. 'Well, that's it then. Probably just an old lumber room or something.'

Millie nodded, but her curiosity was aroused.

Aunt Natalie was frosty over supper, for which they had a delicious kind of Russian stew called goulash. She thawed over their game of scrabble later, however, and things were back to normal by the time they went to bed.

Anna took them to a stables for an early ride the next morning. As they trotted down a woodland lane, Millie told Kevin of the peculiarly vivid dream she'd had during the night.

'There was a ballerina,' she said. 'I couldn't see her face, but she danced beautifully, and she kept beckoning for me to follow her. I must have sleep-walked, because I woke up standing in the middle of the room. I'd stubbed my toe on the wardrobe, you see, and that's what wakened me,'

Kevin laughed. 'You think about nothing else but dancing these days. When you're a professional you'll have to change your name, you know – how about Millicenta Brownovich?'

'Sarcastic – achoo! – clot!' yelled Millie in mock rage as her brother cantered on down the path.

When they came back to Hollydene Avenue, Aunt Natalie was getting ready to go shopping with Anna.

'Are you sure you two won't come along?' she asked.

'No thanks, Aunt,' said Kevin, repressing a shudder. Looking at ladies' hats was not his idea of fun.

When they had gone, Millie slipped out to the corner shop for a large bottle of lemonade. She left it on the coffee-table in the living-room and went into the kitchen where Kevin was piling biscuits on to a plate.

'Can you see any glasses anywhere?' she asked.

'There they are,' said Kevin, reaching a couple of pyrex ones from a shelf. Suddenly there was a splintering crash from the next room. They rushed in to find the bottle in pieces on the floor, and lemonade soaking into the rug.

'You clumsy idiot, Millie! You must have left it right on the edge!'

'I did not!' shouted Millie, 'I put it right in the middle of the table. It must have fallen off by itself!'

'Oh, don't be so silly,' said Kevin angrily. 'It couldn't have!'

A row developed, and by lunchtime they were hardly speaking. Kevin had collected the broken glass and hidden it in the dustbin, and Millie managed to dry the rug fairly well in front of the fire.

They were meant to go to a football match that afternoon, but Millie's hay fever had worsened, so Anna took Kevin to the match and Millie sprawled sulking on a sofa, sneezing, with streaming eyes and a nagging headache. Aunt Natalie started a game of Monopoly with her, but nodded off after a few minutes. Millie fidgeted, bored, and tried to sneeze quietly. Then she had an idea. When she was sure her Aunt was properly asleep, she crept noiselessly out of the room and up the stairs, towards the attic.

Kevin enjoyed his soccer. When they returned, he lingered in the back garden for a few practice kicks on his own. He dribbled the football up and down the path for a few minutes, then aimed a kick at the wall. Unfortunately the ball went wide and travelled straight for the kitchen window. Kevin closed his eyes and clapped his hands over his ears against the expected crash. The ball hit the window with a loud thud and bounced back harmlessly, the window intact. Kevin was astonished. Suddenly a disturbing thought struck him. He walked up to the kitchen window and began to examine it closely.

'Anna,' said Aunt Natalie worriedly, 'I found the children going up to explore the attic yesterday.'

'Oh no!' gasped Anna. 'Did they see inside?'

The old lady shook her head. 'I stopped them on the stairs.'

'Thank goodness for that.' Anna sank into a chair. 'What did you say to them?'

'Simply that there is nothing to interest them. That they must not go to the third storey.'

'But Natalie, hadn't we better tell them about the attic? Warn them?'

'No Anna, I don't think so,' she replied. 'Why disturb their peace of mind?'

'But they may be curious,' argued Anna, 'and attempt another visit.'

Natalie Veronik sighed wearily. 'I think not,' she said. 'There is plenty to occupy them here, and there is no danger during the hours of daylight.' Her lip trembled, and she turned away abruptly.

'My poor Helena. . . .'

Millie and Kevin met up before supper that evening. Both were bursting to tell what they had found out that afternoon, but the morning's quarrel had left them standing on their dignity rather.

It was Kevin who spoke first.

'How's your hay fever?' he asked grudgingly.

'Much better, thanks.'

There was a pause, then they both said together:

'I've got something to tell you!'

'You first,' said Kevin with a grin.

'Well, I went up to the attic this afternoon when Aunt Natalie was asleep, and what do you think? – It's a ballet studio! It must have been Helena's. The floor's wooden, there's a practice bar, and one wall's covered by a huge mirror with a kind of house carved into the glass. It looks like a castle in a fairy tale. There are dozens of books about ballet, some cups and awards, and . . . a wheelchair.'

'A wheelchair?'

'Yes. I suppose Helena must have had an accident or something. But Kevin, it's a perfect place to practise, it's just like Mrs Carson's ballet school at home. I wonder why Aunt Natalie didn't tell us about it? Do you think she'd let me use it if I told her I'm learning to dance?'

Kevin shook his head. 'Mum said not to mention it. Are you sure about the mirror in the attic? Because there's something queer about this house.'

Millie looked bewildered. 'How do you mean?' she asked.

'Well, nothing else here is made of glass.'

'But there are mirrors, and windows. . . .'

'Yes, but they're not ordinary glass. I can't be absolutely sure, of course, but I'm pretty certain that they are a kind of plastic substitute, or that special reinforced glass they use for car windscreens. All the drinking glasses are pyrex, there are no glass ornaments, no television. . . .'

'I see,' said Millie slowly. 'Whenever we've brought glass into the house, your watch, my mirror, that bottle this morning – they're smashed.'

'Exactly,' said Kevin excitedly. 'We have to find out more about Helena Veronik, Millie, because I'm sure it all ties in with her –'

They were interrupted by Anna calling them down to supper.

Later in the evening Aunt Natalie told them amazing stories of her escape to England. Millie and Kevin listened spellbound as she spoke of dangerous incidents, which sounded like television adventures to them, but which were common enough in those desperate years. She talked on, her strangely-accented voice making the tales compelling and real. Her last story was of hiding with Anna in a hayrick, holding their breaths as the tramp of jackboots came nearer, louder . . . then the tremendous relief as the patrol passed by, and the footsteps faded.

'It's just as well we didn't suffer from hay fever, Millie,' smiled Anna.

'Yes indeed,' chuckled their Aunt. 'One sneeze and we surely should have been discovered! Well, all this talking has made me tired, and I must go to bed. Goodnight, my dears.' She kissed them and left the room.

Kevin turned immediately to Anna. 'You and Aunt Natalie have certainly had very exciting lives,' he began.

'Too exciting perhaps, and very sad sometimes,' she replied.

'Will you tell us about Helena, Anna?' asked Millie, moving her chair closer. 'She would have been our cousin if she had lived, wouldn't she?'

Anna stared at them for a few moments, then seemed to make up her mind.

'Very well. Helena Veronik was a dancer,' she began. 'The attic room was converted into a studio for her, and she used to spend nearly all her free time there practising, when she wasn't having lessons. She had a kind of house etched into a mirror up there, and she often used to say that she wished it were real, so that she could live there and dance and dance forever. Well, she was a very gifted dancer, and at sixteen she seemed all set for a brilliant career. Then she fell in love with a worthless man.' Anna frowned at the memory. 'One day she missed a class to go out driving with him in the country, and he drove too recklessly and crashed the car. He was unharmed, but Helena hurt her back and could no longer walk. Her fiancé deserted her, and so she lost everything.'

'That's awful. What happened to her then?' Kevin prompted, as Anna paused.

'Helena used to spend hours in her wheelchair, just staring into the mirror. One day she died. It may have been the result of her spinal injury, or perhaps a broken heart. To Natalie, of course, her daughter's memory is sacred, and that is why she does not wish anyone, ever, to visit the studio. That is all you need to know about Helena, my dears.'

Anna stood up briskly. 'Heavens, look at the time – bed, both of you!'

'Do you think Anna told us everything?' asked Millie, half an hour later. She had crept into her brother's room for a whispered conference as soon as the house was silent. 'Because what she said doesn't really explain the broken glass, does it? Unless . . .' she shuddered. 'Unless there's some sort of a spell on the glass in this house because of the mirror upstairs.'

'Oh, it's probably just a coincidence.' Kevin's attempted laugh sounded hollow.

'But Kevin, what if Helena's still – I mean, if she's. . . .'

'A ghost?' Kevin frowned. 'No, that's impossible. Don't think about it. Even if the house *is* haunted, and I don't believe it is, it can't effect us as long as we don't go near the studio.'

'I suppose not.' Millie yawned. 'Well, I'm going to bed now. Goodnight.'

'Goodnight,' said Kevin. Both of them had quite forgotten Millie's dream of the previous evening.

Towards midnight Kevin woke with a start, and the vague feeling that something was wrong. It was the same sense of unease that he had felt outside the attic door. He tried to ignore it, telling himself that he was imagining things.

Then, very distantly and sweetly, he heard music playing, Tchaikovsky or some such. . . .

Ballet music! In a second Kevin was out of bed and padding to his sister's room. Millie's bed was empty. As quickly and quietly as he could, Kevin ran along the landing and up the stairs towards the attic. The white door was slightly open, and he could see a phosphorescent-like glow from inside.

Cautiously he pushed open the door and entered the studio. The scene before him rooted him to the ground with amazement. The source of the strange light was the mirror, and the turreted house which was carved upon it seemed lit from within by an unearthly glow. Millie, dressed in her tunic and ballet shoes, was standing motionless, her back to him, one hand resting on the practice bar. She seemed to be staring hypnotised at the slender, fragile figure of a ballerina which was dancing slowly before her to the strains of the faint music. Time seemed to have run down, like a slow-motion film, and Kevin could not tell if the dancer was outside the mirror or the mirror had become three-dimensional. The ballerina was deathly white, and lustreless as chalk. She drifted and swayed with the lazy grace of sea-ferns, her eyes blank and dark and fixed upon his sister.

As he watched, the dancer glided over to Millie and took her hands, and stepping backwards pulled her gently towards the eerie light. What would happen when they reached the house of glass? Would they vanish inside forever?

Panic-stricken, Kevin tried to shout, but his throat was tight with fear. Millie was moving like a sleep-walker, ever closer to the haunted mirror. Kevin glanced wildly round, and suddenly noticed a crystal trophy on a table near his hand. Without pausing to think he picked it up and hurled it with all of his strength at the glass.

Instantly the glow faded, the music vanished and the mirror shattered silently, jagged fragments and splinters of glass scattering on to the floor soundlessly, as if they had been autumn leaves. Then the studio was filled with the sound of a great peaceful sigh, and dimly in the moonlight the slight shade sped towards the open window, and was gone.

Kevin ran to Millie, who was curled up on the floor, and shook her urgently. She opened her eyes and sat up, yawning and blinking.

'Morning,' she mumbled drowsily. 'I had *such* a funny dream.' She gazed around vaguely, then stared at Kevin in astonishment. 'What are we doing in here? Who broke the mirror?'

'Sssh! Let's get out of here.'

They crept out of the studio, down to Kevin's room, where he told Millie all that had happened.

'It sounds as if I had a narrow escape,' said Millie gravely, when he had finished. 'I dreamed that Helena was taking me to a kind of fairyland. I didn't know it was all really happening. Why didn't Aunt Natalie warn us?'

'I suppose she thought we were safe enough as long as we didn't go into the studio at night,' said Kevin. 'She didn't know about your ballet lessons, so she couldn't reckon on Helena feeling a kind of bond with you, and wanting to take you with her into the world that imprisoned her, before the house of glass and the spell that bound her were broken.'

Millie shivered. 'I suppose we'll have to tell Aunt Natalie in the morning,' she said.

'Yes, we will,' answered Kevin thoughtfully. 'But I think she will be glad to know that Helena Veronik is free now, and resting peacefully at last.'

This story will appear in *The Ninth Armada Ghost Book,* to be published this spring by Armada Books.

How Your Money Was Spent

Martyn Day

Of all the various projects that we do on Magpie certainly the biggest is the annual Magpie Appeal, when, with your help, we raise money to help handicapped children. Since we started the Appeal in 1969, you have raised many thousands of pounds, all of which has gone to help children with different kinds of handicap.

Work started on the Christmas 1975 Appeal in October when Mick, Doug and Jenny had a big meeting with all the Magpie team to discuss possible Appeal subjects. After a lot of careful discussion it was decided to help a rather unusual group of youth clubs, clubs where physically handicapped and able-bodied children are able to meet.

One of the major problems faced by handicapped children is loneliness and lack of contact with the outside world. Quite often they are confined to a hospital or special school and have little chance to mix with children who are not handicapped. Unlike able-bodied children, they cannot play in the street, or visit the local disco, and so feel cut off from normal everyday activities. The youth clubs that we decided to help can overcome this problem by giving these handicapped children the opportunity to mix with able-bodied children, and take part in normal youth club activities, like table tennis, disco-dancing and visits out to places such as the cinema or the seaside. We discovered that there were nearly 200 of these clubs all over the country, and although they were thriving, they needed a lot of help with transport to get the children to the clubs, special ramps to allow children in wheelchairs to get up steps, and general equipment like games and record players.

We launched the Magpie Appeal on 2 December 1975 when Doug visited a club in Hemsworth, Yorkshire. There he met eleven-year-old John Sayles who is handicapped himself. John told Doug what it is like to be handicapped. 'My problem is that I have no muscles in my legs, and I am unable to walk without the aid of calipers. I don't mind this so much,' John said, 'but it upsets me when people stare . . . they just don't seem to understand.' But in spite of his handicap John is very lively, and he used to get very bored sitting alone at home, until he heard about his local 'Physically Handicapped and Able-Bodied' club. Now he is a very keen member, and takes part in all the games, especially the football, and looks forward to club night every week. John's club in Hemsworth became our first target in the Appeal. Because the club had only just started, it desperately needed basic equipment like a record player, table tennis tables, footballs and art materials. This would cost over £800, and after Mick, Doug and Jenny had set the target, they nervously waited to see if the money would come in.

And of course you didn't let them down. By the end of the first week we had received £7,205, and Mick, Doug and Jenny were able not only to buy the equipment for Hemsworth, but also supply ramps and a store room for another club in Liverpool, and a mini bus to help clubs in the Rhondda Valley of South Wales.

The money just rolled in— by the end of the second week it had reached £29,902, and you had helped over seventeen clubs in all parts of the country. Along with the money came your letters, telling us how you raised the funds. There were the schoolboys in Scotland who had 'kidnapped' their teacher, and held him to ransom! There were the girls who made and sold gingerbread men at a church bazaar. Sixteen-year-old Nigel Burt of Chester even organised a sponsored three-mile canoe race up the River Dee.

On 19 December Doug visited a grand club party in London and amongst the young guests he met Jimmy 'Howzabout that, guys and gals' Savile, and Steve the Human Skeleton, both of whom had come along to meet the kids. Everyone was pleased to hear Doug

announce that the Appeal had reached £46,164. Not bad going for three weeks!

Soon Christmas was upon us, and that meant a lot of work for everyone on the team, and especially Mick, Doug and Jenny. First of all there was the Magpie Christmas Party that took place in one of the London clubs. Jenny demonstrated how to ice a Christmas Cake, and then Doug and Mick demonstrated how *not* to ice a Christmas Cake! There was more icing on the floor than on the cake.

By Christmas Eve the Appeal was really into its stride. Already we had received £62,094, and letters were rolling in at the rate of 5,000 a week! The Magpie correspondence girls, Pat, Marita and Marion, disappeared behind a wall of mail and red-hot typewriters as they got down to the job of replying. On 30 December the

Appeal had reached £67,370, and Mick, Doug and Jenny were able to announce that we had been able to help 73 clubs so far. On that programme the new target was for a mini bus for the Bristol and Avon area, to help encourage new clubs in the region.

The mini buses that we were buying were rather special, each one being converted to meet the requirements of the club that it would belong to. Basically they started out as a normal 17-cwt van, the kind that you might see carrying goods in any High Street. Then coachbuilders cut off and raised the roof to allow people to stand up inside, and cut holes in the side panels for windows. Seats were added inside, making sure that there was room for wheelchairs to be stored. And to finish the bus off a hoist was added on the back so that people in

wheelchairs could get in without being lifted.

As we moved into the new year the Appeal had reached an incredible £85,933, and Mick, Doug and Jenny started to think that you might just break the record £91,000 set in the previous year's Appeal. It did really seem as if you were all doing your best to help. One boy offered to crawl from London to Brighton to raise money. In another project two boys from Selby in Yorkshire broke the world hopscotch record on the Appeal's behalf. We even received some money from the crew of H.M.S. *Leander*, one of the Navy ships patrolling the troubled waters off Iceland. They raffled a bar of chocolate! Of course the three presenters were busy as well. Doug visited a social club in Tonbridge to pick up some money, and amazed everyone, including himself, by playing a solo on the club drum kit. Mick played in an Appeal Football Match with the Showbiz 11, and Jenny got thrown around in a Judo Marathon!

In January Mick, Doug and Jenny set two new targets, one to provide transport and equipment for clubs in Scotland, at Dundee, Selkirk, Edinburgh and Glasgow. (When the Appeal started we had been able to find only one club in Scotland, but Scottish viewers gave us a lot of help to find more, and we were pleased to be able to help them all.) The other target was for Belfast, in Northern Ireland. They needed a mini bus to enable more handicapped children to get to the club. The Belfast club is the only one in the Province at present, so as you can imagine there are lots of

members. But unfortunately it is difficult for many of the more handicapped members to get to the club, so the mini bus will come in most useful. When Mick visited the club himself he met sixteen-year-old Keith Brown who has invented a special electronic switch to help his severely handicapped friends to operate TV games, and electric typewriters. Keith hopes to get his invention patented, so it should help handicapped people all over the world!

By now we were on the last leg of the Appeal, and the big question was, 'Would we reach £100,000 before the Appeal finished on January 23?' On Friday 16 January it had reached £93,520, and everyone on the team had their fingers crossed. Of course Mick, Doug and Jenny were delighted that you had broken the £91,000 total of the year before, but as they said, 'It would be good to finish on a nice round figure.' During the last week the letters poured in, 600 one day, 400 the next. . . . The red line slowly inched forward . . . £97,000 and then £98,000. On the last two days over 1,000 letters came in, and were quickly opened and counted. Had we reached £100,000? The newspapers phoned in to find out the news. 'Had we done it?' But there was strict secrecy in the office. The first people to find out had to be the very people who had so generously donated, Magpie viewers themselves.

And then came the final day, 23 January 1976. In the studio Mick and Jenny were helping to arrange some of the tons of equipment that they had been able to buy for the clubs: record players, table tennis

and archery games, braille draught and chess sets, painting materials, a potter's wheel, a mini bus still being converted—the list went on and on. Outside in the corridor the red line was being laid in place. Everyone wanted to know how much the Appeal had raised.

The red light came on for transmission of the programme. Mick said, 'We have some good news on the Appeal.' Over the studio doors a ribbon was being fixed in place; did this mean that you had done it?

Well, of course, you had. At the end of the programme Mick and Jenny together cut the ribbon and stepped into the studio. As they did, they announced the final figure. Not £100,000, but a truly amazing £107,213·72! The largest amount ever collected for a Magpie Appeal. It all added up to eight mini buses, and literally tons of other equipment for 'Physically Handicapped and Able-Bodied' clubs all over the country, from Dundee to the Isle of Wight, from Belfast to Cardiff, giving thousands of handicapped children the chance to broaden their horizons, to make new friends and discover new interests. Equally it means that able-bodied children now have a real opportunity to learn about some of the problems that handicapped children face.

But even after the Appeal had closed money still came in from long-term projects, and after it was all added up, it brought the Grand Total up to over £125,000!

So the Appeal was over, at least for another year. All that was left to do was to thank all of you for your

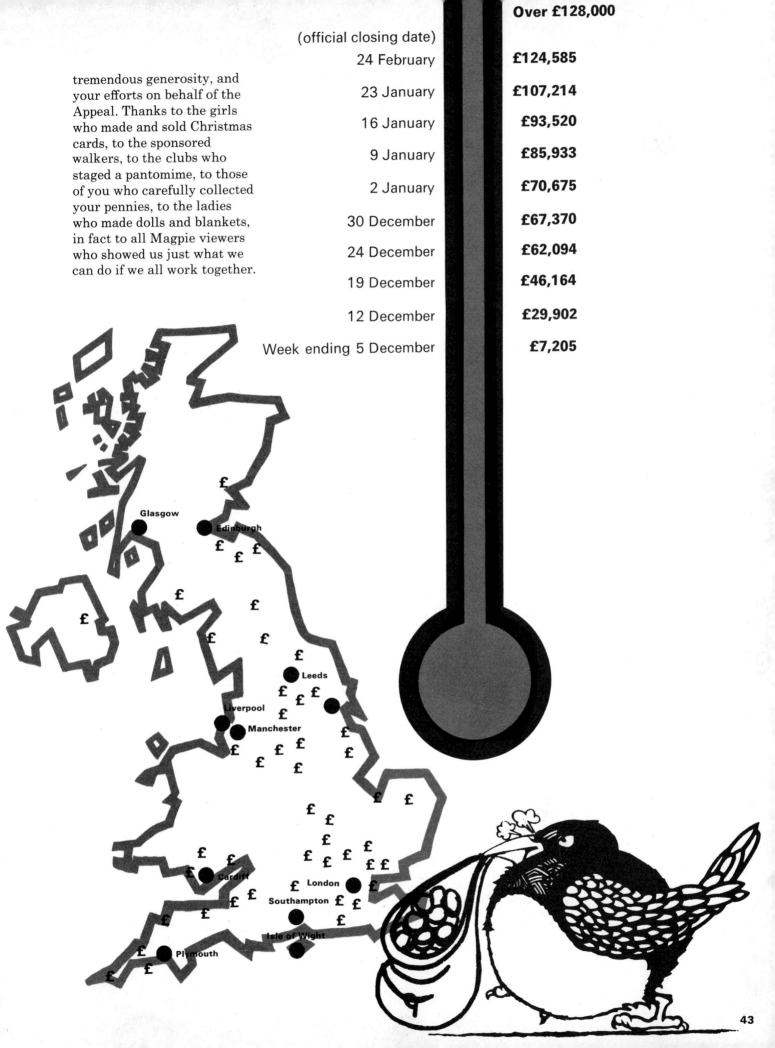

tremendous generosity, and your efforts on behalf of the Appeal. Thanks to the girls who made and sold Christmas cards, to the sponsored walkers, to the clubs who staged a pantomime, to those of you who carefully collected your pennies, to the ladies who made dolls and blankets, in fact to all Magpie viewers who showed us just what we can do if we all work together.

	Over £128,000
(official closing date)	
24 February	£124,585
23 January	£107,214
16 January	£93,520
9 January	£85,933
2 January	£70,675
30 December	£67,370
24 December	£62,094
19 December	£46,164
12 December	£29,902
Week ending 5 December	£7,205

Glasgow
Edinburgh
Leeds
Liverpool
Manchester
Cardiff
London
Southampton
Isle of Wight
Plymouth

FISHY FACTS

Recently Jenny has been spending some time learning how to fish on Magpie. Here are some facts that we did not tell you on the series:

The *largest* fish in the world is the rare plankton-feeding Whale Shark. This fish is found in the warmer parts of the Atlantic, Pacific and Indian Oceans. In 1919 a Whale Shark which was 59 feet in length and weighed over 42 tons, was trapped in a bamboo stake-trap in the Gulf of Siam.

In April 1959 a man-eating Great White Shark measuring 16 feet 10 inches was caught off the coast of Australia. This was the *largest* fish that has ever been caught on a *rod*.

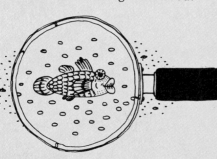

The *fastest* fish in the world is the Sailfish. Although it is very difficult to measure the speed at which a fish swims, speeds of up to 68 miles per hour are recorded for this fish.

The *most venomous* fish in the world are the Stonefish. They are found in the tropical waters of the Indo-Pacific. Direct contact with the spines of these fish often proves fatal.

The *largest carnivorous* fish is the Great White Shark (also called the 'Maneater'), which is found in tropical and sub-tropical water. In June 1930 a specimen 37 feet long was trapped in a Herring weir in New Brunswick, Canada.

The *smallest* fish in the world is a Marshall Island Goby which measures between 12 and 16 millimetres. This fish is found in the Pacific Ocean and weighs about 2 milligrammes. (That means you would need to catch 17,750 of these fish to weigh 1 ounce!)

A Common Sturgeon weighing nearly 500 pounds was caught in Yorkshire in 1810. This was the *biggest* fish ever caught in a British river.

The *oldest* fish in the world is a Lake Sturgeon which was caught in Ontario, Canada in 1953—it was believed to be 154 years old.

White goldfish have been reputed to live for over 40 years in China. The *oldest* British goldfish was probably 29 years, 10 months, 21 days when it died in April 1883.

TOTTERS

THAMES TELEVISION
PROD MAGPIE "TOTTER"
DIRECTOR P. YOLLAND   CAMERAMAN M. RHODES
SLATE 13   TAKE 2
12TH FEBRUARY   DAY-EXT

Mitcham is a busy and expanding suburb of London, but overlooked by industrial plant and half-built modern flats, is a small yard with rickety old stables and four ponies. This is where Tommy the Totter has his headquarters and where his family have worked for generations before him. And it is where Mick and a Magpie film crew assembled one rainy, rainy day last February.

Tommy, of course, is a rag and bone man. Researcher Kate Marlow had met him a couple of weeks before the filming day and he had agreed to take Mick out on one of his rounds so that you could see what the work of a rag and bone man is like.

The first thing to do was to harness up Joey, Tommy's four-year-old Apalucian pony. Ponies still compare favourably with vans as a means of transport because although the cost of food and shoes is always rising, it is less than the price of petrol, road tax and insurance. Ponies are good for business, too, because customers like them and they travel at a suitable pace. And a well-trained pony like Joey can keep going on his own while the Totter is knocking on doors.

Joey had been specially groomed for Magpie's visit, his tail neatly bound up with straw and pink ribbons. Mick helped Tommy put on the red-tongued harness and then back the pony into the scalloped and painted cart which is known as a 'trolley'.

Filming wasn't easy — the rain didn't stop for a second and the camera and the sound equipment had to be wrapped up in polythene bags for protection. There was quite an audience in the small yard, for several of Tommy's relations live there in smart modern caravans, and they watched the proceedings, dodging out of the view of the camera as it followed Mick and Tommy.

Tommy confessed that he wouldn't normally go out on a day like this, but since Magpie wasn't daunted, he wasn't going to be either. So the traffic outside the yard was stopped and Joey swung out into the road and up to the centre of Mitcham.

To give you a bird's eye view of the pony and trolley amidst the busy traffic, Magpie had got special permission to go inside the disused Majestic cinema and film from its high windows. So while Mick and Tommy circled Upper Green the film crew, by this time drenched, lugged their equipment up the eerie shell of the Majestic.

As Mick and Tommy trotted smartly up London Road towards the cinema, director Peter Yolland shouted 'Action!' and the camera whirred. Something had gone wrong, though. Mike Rhodes, the cameraman, was pretty sure he hadn't got the best shot. So round the green went Mick and Tommy once more and there was another 'take'.

Everyone was very wet, cold and hungry by this time, so while the sound recordist recorded some traffic noise to serve as background for the film, Tommy and his brother Dave took Joey back to the stables. And everyone met up in a restaurant for a hot lunch. Over the meal, Tommy gave Mick some information about his work and life, which Mick would use later in the week when he recorded the commentary to the film. Tommy explained that Totters were originally gypsies who settled in Mitcham at the turn of the century. Tommy is descended from the most famous of them, the Sparrowhawks.

About a dozen Totters still work in Mitcham, although not all of them use ponies. Tommy has worked in the business almost literally his whole life — when he was just a child he used to go out on the trolley with his Grandad.

His main source of income today comes from scrap iron. Rags are not worth so much and most old furniture is a waste of time. All the same, Tommy will buy almost anything for which he thinks he might get a price. The 'Steptoe' image that rag and bone men have is quite wrong, according to Tommy : 'Only a nut would collect false teeth', he said, and besides, the Totter's aim is to make a living, so he sells everything as fast as he can and doesn't hoard it. When business is bad, Tommy keeps the business ticking over by selling horse manure. In the old days, Totters used to sell vinegar, and they collected bones to be melted down.

Mick asked Tommy what happened to the scrap and rags once he'd collected them. The scrap iron, Tommy explained, is sold to a yard in Mitcham. It then goes to Wales where it is melted down and re-used. The rags are sterilised and the white ones are separated from the coloured rags. Some are exported to be used for industrial cleaning and some are used as polishing rags by garages in this country.

Everyone had thawed out during lunch and

it was with some reluctance that they all
trooped out into the rain again. The plan now
was to visit some houses and do a bit of
buying. A cul-de-sac had been chosen for
the first visit, so that main-road traffic would
not get in the way. The idea was to film Mick
and Tommy trotting up to the cul-de-sac,
hollering a Totter's cry. So while they waited
round the corner, the crew climbed onto the
Thames van to make sure they got a good
view.

When everything was ready, Peter Yolland
shouted 'Action', and Joey clip-clopped up
the road, with Mick and Tommy yelling 'Any
old lumber! Any old lumber!'

Sure enough, a housewife popped out and
said she had an old sofa and a few other
odds and ends that she'd like to be taken
away. Joey was given a tray of corn while
Tommy went to inspect the goods. He said
he wouldn't normally buy a sofa but agreed
to do so for the film. So he and Mick started
loading the stuff onto the trolley. There
seemed to be an enormous amount and
when the sequence was over, the housewife
pointed out that several items that she
hadn't wanted to sell had been loaded up.
This posed a problem: if it was taken off,
would viewers notice that it was missing in
the next sequence of the film? If so, the
loading-up would have to be re-shot. It was
decided no one would notice and the extra
goods were returned to their owner.

Next, some close-ups were needed, so the
cameraman and sound recordist clambered
on to the trolley and Joey pulled them all to
the next chosen street.

By the time a few more calls had been
made, the light was beginning to fade and it
was becoming clear that the plan to visit the
scrap yard to see what happened to Tommy's
takings, would have to be scrapped. To
clinch this, Mike the cameraman fell off the
trolley and, probably because water had got
inside it, the camera exploded.

It had been a cold, wet day, and no one
was at all sure that enough film had been
made to make a story. Still, Tommy had
remained cheerful and kept everyone's spirits
up. And Mick found he had enjoyed his day
in spite of the rain and had learnt a lot about
the Totter's trade, particularly that it is
carried out in a very businesslike manner and
that in these days of scarce raw materials, it
is a very useful trade.

NESSIE

'An object of considerable dimensions rose out of the water not so far from where I was. I did not see a head for what I took to be the front parts were under the water, but there was considerable movement in what appeared to be the tail. . . .'

'I noticed a considerable commotion on the surface some distance out, perhaps two or three hundred yards out, and saw something break the surface. . . . "My God," my friend shouted, "it's the monster."'

'I was able to make out clearly the monster's head which was like that of a goat. On top of the head were two stumps resembling sheep's horns broken off. The neck was about 40 feet long, its colour was between nigger and dark brown. The skin appeared to be smooth, the markings of a lizard. The animal appeared to have flippers on the fore part of the body and these were extended straight forward and not being used. The eyes were slits like that of a darning needle, it was moving at about 8 mph, there was no wash or commotion. The length of the body was 20 feet. . . .'

'It looked like a hump then another two humps appeared. The three humps were visible all the time and in the front of them was a long thin neck and head about the size and shape of a sheep's head. Its head and neck kept bobbing down into the water. . . .'

'Something appeared about 50 yards away on my port bow. It seemed to be swimming very steadily and converging on me. It looked like a very large flat head four or five feet long and wide. I was convinced it was the head and neck of a very large creature. . . . I simply could not believe it. . . .'

You've guessed! All the writers above were talking about the Loch Ness monster. St Columba is the first person who thought he saw a monster in the Loch. That was in AD 565 and *still* there is controversy about the creature.

Last year, Magpie asked you to send in your own ideas of Nessie. Nearly 10,000 of you went in for the competition. Here are some of the prizewinners' drawings, plus a few more which went on display at Thames Television in the Euston Road.

Barry McGuiness (14)

LOCH NESS MONSTER. Graeme Heaton, 15, School Lane, Lostock Hall. Preston PRS 5JS Lancs. AGE 4 yrs.

Sara Jane Goddard (8), **1st prize**

UNDER 11'S

Kerry Bailham (10), **equal 3rd prize**

Celia Dibbs (9)

Louis Longhi (5), **equal 3rd prize**

Grahame Dye (14), **1st prize**

Estelle Bishop (13)

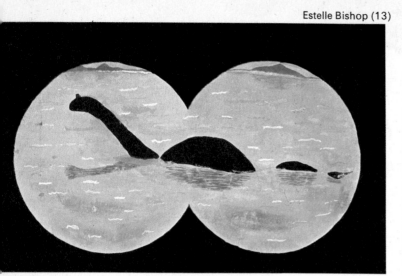

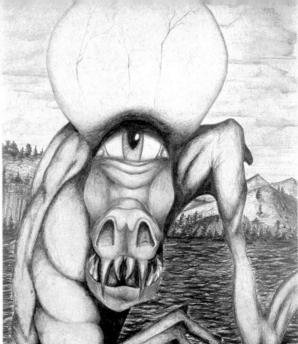

11 AND OVER

Philip Knightley (12)

Roy Springhall (15), **2nd prize**

Anonymous

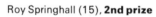

Andrew Hazel (14), **3rd prize**

Have fun with yeast
The bread recipe on page 12 contains no yeast. But yeast is fun because it is alive and you can watch it grow. It is much easier to use than you might think, and you can use it in all sorts of bread, as well as in buns and doughnuts and lardy cakes and other delicious bready things.

OWZAT!

Last year Mick and Doug formed part of a cricket team captained by Frank Bough of 'Grandstand' which challenged Michael Barrett's 'Nationwide' team to a charity match. It was held at Maidenhead and despite a lot of rain there was a big crowd.

. . . he took two for fourteen and surprised everyone . . .

Michael Barrett was an early batsman and he got a few runs before he hit his stumps.

including himself.

And Michael Parkinson took the game very seriously.

During the interval Mick and Doug had a chance to sign autographs . . .

When it was Mick's turn to bowl . . .

for the hundreds of children who turned up to watch the match.

And they met Valerie Singleton who was a spectator.

Then it was time for Frank Bough's team to bat.

Michael Parkinson scored a very fine eighty-five runs which gave his side a good chance of winning.

Then Frank Bough scored twelve runs.

Doug got, well, six.

Then he swapped with Mick . . .

who scored ten not out and his team won by two wickets.

Mick and Doug aren't going to make the England team, but they enjoyed their innings – and so did the crowd!

$\mathcal{P}$resenting

It's practically impossible to get a word in edgeways to either Jenny, Doug or Mick, let alone talk to all three together. One or other of them is almost always out filming or dubbing or visiting somewhere. But they wanted to show you their Magpie photographs and to talk to you in this year's *Annual*, so they took a tape recorder with them on the train to Southampton and recorded some reminiscences for you. Train noise blurred a lot of their conversation but this is what we could hear above the chuffing.

Douglas: One of the great things about being a Magpie presenter is the opportunity we get of doing all sorts of things that would be impossible if we had normal jobs. Travel, for instance. Over the past few years Magpie has been to Holland, Lebanon, Hong Kong, the Philippines, France, America, Iran, Kenya, Morocco, Switzerland and Malta. We sometimes have slight language problems when

abroad. I remember in Morocco I had to ride with some tribesmen in a charge called the Fantasia. I didn't realise you had to speak Arabic to the horses and when the director said 'Cue, Douglas', all the tribesmen started charging towards the cameraman and I was left on the starting line because I didn't know the Arabic word for making horses go.

Mick: I think some of our most disastrous moments have happened abroad. On my first trip abroad with Magpie, to Kenya, we were interviewing a game warden in a National Park when suddenly we heard a trampling noise of breaking trees and an elephant appeared in the clearing with his ears outstretched, galloping towards us. We all ran like mad, leaving the camera behind. Luckily the elephant didn't harm the camera, nor did he catch us so it all ended OK – but it was a close shave.

Jenny: We had that same camera when we were in France and had a near disaster. It was a beautiful day in the Camargue, which is a very boggy area, and we were herding horses, riding bareback. When we finished filming we put the camera and other equipment in a boat and then we all piled in. The boat was very overladen and as we pushed it ashore it started to sink. Luckily we found the camera and threw it onto a little island. Then we had to rescue the sound technician who had equipment round his neck and was being dragged under. Finally we were all safe and rushed back to the hotel and dried out the camera with hair dryers. We thought that the whole day's filming was probably ruined – and there was no time to film it all over again – but it was all right and we were able to show it on Magpie. I think that camera is jinxed: if it comes on another summer trip it's going straight out of the window!

Douglas: Well it was the same camera again that we took to America and then it *did* go out of the window. We had a wonderful time going from coast to coast, and we stopped for just over a week in the Grand Canyon. One night, at about two in the morning, people heard a noise outside their motel bedroom doors. They discovered the place was on fire. It was a new motel, made of wood, and soon the whole building was ablaze.

Mick: Yes, there was considerable chaos, with people running hither and thither while the equipment was being got out. The camera assistant was stuck in his room so he smashed the window and threw that rotten camera out. It landed safely but the poor camera assistant was badly cut on his arm and had to come home. Everyone on Magpie was all right in the end, but all the film was burnt and we had to make it over again.

Jenny: Some of the disastrous things that happen are very funny when you look back on them. I remember my very first programme I had to show how to make a puppet and I stabbed myself with a pin and my finger started bleeding. Then I couldn't get the puppet off my hand but you two couldn't help me because you were on Newsdesk and anyway you were just giggling at me. Finally, I leant on the top of the Make and Do desk and the whole thing collapsed!

Douglas: I remember a funny Make and Do, too. Mick and I were preparing an apple pie. All the ingredients were ready and I was about to put it in the oven when you came over, Jenny, and said, 'Haven't you forgotten something?' I'd forgotten to put the apples in the pie!

Mick: Funny things often happen with animals. Do you remember when we had white mice on the programme? I was just saying what delightful, well-behaved little creatures they were when one of them sunk its teeth into me and held on and actually drew blood.

Jenny: Yes, and last summer we had that baby kitten on the programme. Unfortunately someone had overturned its waterbowl. I lifted the kitten onto my knees and had wet trousers for the rest of the programme. I remember my first film, too – I was told I had to spend a day at London Zoo looking after a baby. I didn't realise it was going to be a baby elephant. It was huge and kept putting its trunk down my wellington boot.

Douglas: There are lots of things, though, that are memorable not because they are funny or disastrous but because they are wonderful or strange experiences. The time in Iran, for instance, when we spent a few days filming a nomadic tribe. We had a party when the filming was over and they presented us with cups of red liquid. We were told it was bull's blood and we had to drink it or we would have offended them greatly.

Mick: Shooting the rapids through the Colorado River in the Grand Canyon was one of the most exciting experiences I have had on the programme. We did it on an inflatable raft. Tourists can do this now – you get strapped in and go bumping down the river, rather like being on a bucking bronco.

Douglas: Flying over the Grand Canyon in a helicopter was an incredible experience, too. To start with you are flying about 100 feet above the ground; then suddenly you are over the Canyon and about a mile above ground, and the view is absolutely beautiful.

Jenny: Talking about helicopters, one of my most memorable experiences was when I went to Portsmouth and learned what to do if you crash over water in a helicopter. I had to get in a metal box, wearing a helmet and protective clothing, and I was strapped in. You see the water coming towards you and you go under and twist for what seems like ages. Then someone taps on the box when the blades have stopped revolving and you get out and kick your way to the surface. Very painful on the ears!

Mick: I actually did crash once – when I was hang-gliding. I had to run like hell so that the wind got hold of my parachute. I went up about 300 feet, then fell to earth very quickly. I hurt myself so Jenny is going to do all the flying on the programme in future!

Jenny: I'm terrified of flying. Poor Mick, though, it was a very bad crash – you almost broke your neck.

Douglas: To get back to pleasanter matters: I think one of the best things about being a presenter on Magpie is the opportunity one has of meeting famous people, and people who are real experts in their field. I'm very keen on squash, sailing and riding and on Magpie I've not only been able to meet Jonah Barrington, Robin Knox Johnston and David Broome, but I've also tried out their boats and horses – and played squash with Barrington (he won!).

Mick: Yes, on Magpie we get a chance to do things we have always dreamt of doing and that other people might fantasise about but don't get the opportunity to do.

Jenny: It's a tremendous lot of hard work – not just for us but for all the technicians, producers and researchers and so on who work on the programme – but it's tremendous fun, too.

Douglas: I suppose really if one were to sum up the secret of the thrill of being a Magpie presenter it's like placing yourself in a Peter Pan situation where you never grow old or bored but are always faced with the challenge of exciting and interesting things to do. And one of the best things is getting letters from millions of viewers who are interested in the programme and in what we do and want to find out more about particular items.

Jenny: Another thing that's marvellous is the amazing response of viewers to the Appeal. Newspapers say people are becoming meaner, but last year's Appeal proved that it is just not true.

Mick: Yes, the Appeal shows what a large and generous audience we have got. It's the most satisfying single thing that happens to any of us on the programme – to get proof that our viewers care about people who they consider are not as well off as themselves.

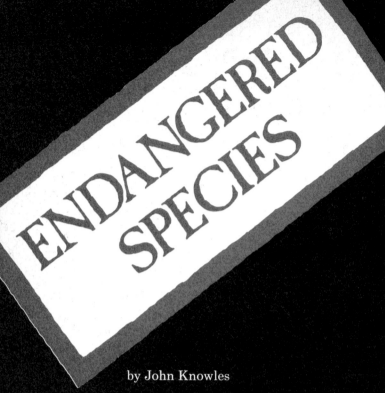

ENDANGERED SPECIES

by John Knowles

Why are some species 'endangered'?

'Dead as a dodo' is an expression you use when you mean that something is absolutely finished for evermore. That is what happened to the dodo, a friendly bird that lived on the island of Mauritius until the seventeenth century. It couldn't fly and was slow to move on land, and was an easy prey for early settlers who killed dodos for meat. Those that were left were destroyed by the dogs, cats and rats that came with the settlers.

The dodo is only the most famous species that is dead and gone, never to return. Since 1771, fifty-five species of animals are known to have become extinct, and there are an unknown number of other species that are extinct in the wild, or that exist only in captivity. And today there are 510 separate species of mammals and birds classified as 'endangered'.

Last year on Magpie, I told you about some of the animals that today are endangered species—animals that do still survive but which are in danger of becoming as dead as the dodo. In a minute I'll mention some of these species by name. But first of all, why are some animals in danger of extinction?

One reason is that the number of human beings is growing enormously. That means that more and more land throughout the world is being taken away from animals for use by humans. We grow *our* food where once animals grazed, and animals lose their habitats; they no longer have places to feed and find water. And they die.

Another reason why some animals face extinction is that they are hunted by men— sometimes for sport, just for the 'fun' of collecting an animal's head or skin—or, more often, for the parts of the animals' bodies that give man something he needs. Whales, for example, are killed for their oil, elephants for their ivory, and rhinoceroses for their horn.

Does it matter?

Do you think it matters if animals become extinct? I think it matters very much, for many reasons. I'll mention just two. The first one is a matter of fact; the second, a matter of opinion on which you must make up your own minds.

First then, *I know* that all species of animal *should* be kept alive because of the 'cycle of nature'. Each species of animal, including human beings, depends on every other one. Take the antelope for instance. The antelope needs grass or bushes to live on, and these will have grown with the help of the plant food which exists in the droppings and carcasses of other animals. These remains are turned into plant food for dozens of insects and other tiny creatures, who in turn are food for still other animals, while the antelope will itself one day be food, having probably been killed by a large flesh-eating animal such as a lion or a leopard. Then what is left will be eaten by still other animals and the vultures will clean up the carcass, so making sure that not too much rotting flesh is left for flies and other insects to eat and increase their numbers too much.

So the cycle goes on, with every animal dependent on another in a perfectly devised system. Although this is not fully understood, it is certain that mankind is also dependent on this complicated process, the cycle of life, and would not be able to survive in a totally human world.

My second reason for saying that animals should not become extinct, is that I feel it would be such a pity if an animal which could exist, *did not*. Can you imagine how sad you would feel if the very last tiger had died and neither you nor your children would ever be able to marvel at the power, grace and beauty of these animals except by seeing pictures or stuffed tigers in a museum?

How can you help?
There are many ways in which you and your friends can help save these animals from extinction. The first is quite simply this: make as many people as possible concerned about animals that are endangered. Do this by learning as much as possible about these animals. Read books, watch wild-life programmes on television, do school projects, and visit zoos where endangered species are bred. And tell your friends about these animals and the dangers they face. Don't buy products which are made from endangered animals, such as fur, souvenirs, foodstuffs, and other articles made from animals.

You can also help animals by giving to, and collecting for, organisations dedicated to saving wild life, such as the World Wildlife Fund, the Fauna Preservation Society, the Royal Society for the Protection of Birds, Marwell Zoological Society's Operation Snow Leopard Fund, and the Wildfowl Trust.

For many animals, there is no longer any chance that they can be saved in the wild, but they may continue in captivity and be happy.

Here again, you can help by finding out which zoos keep and breed endangered animals, and supporting these zoos by visiting them with your friends and families and school parties. A well-run zoo has a much more serious purpose than merely to exhibit animals and you can choose these for your visits rather than those that are simply amusement centres.

It has been a great pleasure for us at Marwell Zoological Park to work with the Magpie team to produce a series on endangered species. We have been very encouraged by the interest so many of you have shown in the series, for with all of you joining the conservation crusade we can do much to ensure the future of endangered species.

Scimitar Horned Oryx
This is one of the most graceful of the group of animals known as *antelope* of which there are many species in Africa, two in Asia and some near cousins who are somewhere between goats and antelope also in Asia, with one of these (known as the Rocky Mountain Goat) in North America. Like deer and cattle, antelope have four stomachs, and because they chew their food a second time, after it has been in their first stomach, are called *ruminants*. Unlike deer, however, but like cattle, antelope only grow one set of horns during their lifetime, and if they are damaged or broken they will not grow again. With most species of antelope only the male grows horns, but with a group known as *hippotraginae* (nothing whatever to do with hippos!) both sexes have horns.

This is the case with the Scimitar Horned Oryx, which carries one of the finest sets of horns of any antelope. These horns sweep backwards from their head in a shape like that of the Arab sword known as a scimitar. These horns are so beautiful that we chose an oryx head as the symbol of Marwell Zoological Park.

Their natural home is the vast semi-desert edges of the Sahara desert known as the Sahelian regions. Plants and small (or scrub) trees can grow there, but recently the droughts have been severe, and overgrazing by domestic animals such as goats has been considerable. Vegetation has been lost, the desert has grown larger and the areas able to support the oryx have decreased.

The Scimitar Horned Oryx unfortunately has another, more dangerous enemy: men armed with powerful rifles and motor vehicles, anxious to have the beautiful horns as a 'trophy', and the flesh of the animal to eat. Many of the hunters are Europeans living in these countries and working on the extraction of minerals. Whenever the deep freeze is empty, bang! there goes another oryx.

Fortunately for the species, these animals have thrived with us in Hampshire and in the last four years over 40 have been born at Marwell, and some born here have themselves produced youngsters. From these some have gone on to form new groups in other zoos around the world. As there is little effective control of poaching in the large tracts of semi-desert where they live, their fortune depends more and more on captive breeding groups such as ours.

Like most desert antelope their colour patterns are designed to camouflage them by a combination of dark and light areas which blend into their brilliant and hot desert backgrounds. The Scimitar Horned Oryx is largely white, with rust-red markings on its front limbs and head. When first born, babies are light brown to enable them to remain hidden if lying still on the ground, which they do until they are strong enough to keep up with the herd. The height at the shoulders of an adult Scimitar Horned Oryx is about 120 cm. They can travel very fast and when pleased with life adopt a remarkable high-stepping trot, a little like that of a hackney horse.

Because from some angles the oryx looks as though it has only one horn, it is thought to be the origin of the legend of the unicorn. Let us hope the Scimitar Horned Oryx will never be a legend of the past.

Przewalski Horse

The Przewalski Wild Horse is one of the most important animals that any zoo can have in its care. We don't know if any of these animals exist in their wild home today, which is a rather cold desert area on the borders of China and Mongolia. But if there are any still living there, it is certain that they are too few to have a real chance of survival.

So it is very lucky that early this century, some of these animals were caught and established in captivity. From a small number, the world population in zoos has gradually increased and in 1975 there were 244. This is still too few for safety if you consider that less than a third of them are females able to produce foals. Marwell's herd was started in 1969 and has grown progressively, with some of the females, themselves born in the zoo, now producing foals.

The Przewalski is the only truly wild horse left in the world today. (Horses that we sometimes think of as wild, like the Mustangs of North America, are descended from domesticated horses. The correct term for animals like these is 'feral', meaning 'gone wild'.) The Przewalski is in fact a species completely separate from any domestic horse. Breeds of domestic horse as different as the massive Shire horse and the tiny Shetland pony are more like each other than either of them is to the Przewalski.

The Przewalski is the size of a large pony, measuring about 14 hands. That is, it measures about 56 inches from the ground to the base of the neck. A characteristic of these horses is their stiff erect mane, and lack of forelock. In winter they grow long yellowish-brown coats, while in summer they have short, paler ones. If you look closely at a Przewalski in summer, you will see black bars on its legs up to its knees, rather like the markings on a zebra.

Study these animals carefully whenever you have a chance to do so, and you will find that they are far more interesting than the rather 'ugly pony' you may have thought them to be at first sight.

Addax

Like the Scimitar Horned Oryx, the addax is
both a member of the *hippotraginae* family,
and a semi-desert living animal, although it is
better able to withstand true desert conditions
than the oryx.

The horns of both the male and the female are
lyre-shaped and the animals themselves are
shorter than the Scimitar Horned Oryx,
standing 104 cm at the shoulder. They have less
white on their bodies and the darker parts are
more of a smoky-grey colour than those of the
oryx. They have rather broad feet in relation to
their size, which is an adaptation for walking
on sand. Below the base of the horns they have a
thick tuft of dark hair which sometimes gives
them the appearance of wearing a wig. In the
wild they live in herds of about twenty animals,
and move over large areas of land in search of
food. So well adapted are they for desert living
that they can manage without any water other
than that which they derive from green food!

Addax are among the most endangered of all
antelope, for all the reasons that the Scimitar
Horned Oryx are endangered, but their problem
is rather worse because they are not as speedy
as the oryx. The pair at Marwell are the only
ones at present in Britain.

The Siberian Tiger

You may be surprised to know that there are
eight races or sub-species of tiger, and each of
these is as different from each other as, for
instance, different breeds of domestic cat are.
Present-day tigers had a prehistoric ancestor
rather like the great sabre-toothed tiger of the
northern, colder areas of the world. Gradually,
as they moved southwards, they became smaller,
with darker coats and thinner stripes, because a
smaller animal coloured in this way is best
able to survive in the hot jungles of Asia. The
smallest of the tiger races is the Javan and the
largest is the Siberian. An adult male Siberian
may weigh as much as 660 lb, or 300 kg.

You have seen on Magpie all but three of the
Siberian tigers born or kept at Marwell Park,
starting with Miko (who is known as Tigger by
his friends). Tigger was the first cub born and
my wife and I reared him, as his mother Nimana
was too inexperienced to do it herself. Because
of this he is particularly friendly with humans
and the television film unit were able to come
right into his cage.

A year after Tigger's birth his mother had
three more cubs and his Aunt Amaga had two,
all of whom were reared by their mothers.
Usually in zoos a female tiger and her cubs

are kept on their own until the cubs are old enough to leave their mother, but because of Amaga and Nimana's friendship and their liking for Kurten, the father of all the cubs, and because we who look after them are also on such good terms with them all, we decided to try something unusual and let them all be together, and this worked very well indeed; a happier family you never saw.

Magpie viewers took part in naming these cubs and the names chosen were Caesar, Jason, Samson, and Tomsk (boys) and Katya (girl). These have all grown up and gone to good homes in other zoos, and Amaga and Nimana have since had more cubs which you saw on Magpie.

Unfortunately, man has hunted Siberian tigers to the point where there are probably no more than 150 left in the wild. Luckily, they have bred well in zoos and there are now about 350 in captivity, of which twelve are at Marwell. It is to be hoped that one day some of these magnificent animals may be returned to their natural homes. . . .

Of the eight races of tiger, all are endangered. One is probably already extinct and two races are so low in numbers that they are likely to become so. Let us hope that the Siberian at least will long continue to share our planet.

White Tailed Gnu

At first sight the White Tailed Gnu is not an attractive animal. He looks a bit like a member of the cattle family gone wrong, although he is in fact an antelope. Like his larger cousins, the Brindled and the White Bearded Gnus, the White Tailed Gnu is well adapted for life on the grassy plains of Africa, where, living in herds, he can travel fast with a movement rather like the canter of a horse, his shoulders considerably higher than his hind legs. An interesting feature of these animals' faces is a flap that covers their nostrils. This helps keep out the dust of the plains when, in the dry season, the herds may travel fast leaving trails of dust behind them. This adds little to their beauty, but is, of course, rather a good idea.

Unlike most antelope, which are silent, they frequently call with a not very tuneful loud snort which the Hottentots of South Africa interpret as a 't'gnu' and hence their name. Their home was once the central plateau of South Africa where they fed on grasses and the succulent buds and leaves of some shrubs, and they often lived in company with a now extinct animal called the Quagga which looked like a zebra without stripes.

The Quagga and the White Tailed Gnu were shot by the early settlers in South Africa for meat and skins and to give more room for farm animals, but a few of the gnu managed to survive, and are still to be found on a few farms and reserves in South Africa and in zoos where their numbers are increasing once again. This is a species for whom the future looks reasonably hopeful, although they no longer exist as a truly wild animal in the sense that they are free to roam over large areas.

Our three gnus at Marwell have to have very strong fences to contain them and the keepers must be very careful of them. Because of the noise they make, visitors have no difficulty in finding where they are!

POLICE CADETS

'The objective of police work is to prevent and detect crime, maintain law and order and preserve the liberty and property of the individual . . . Police work concerns people – their problems, their failings, their daily round.' That's what the Metropolitan Police say their work is all about. It sounds interesting, so Jenny went along to the cadet school at Hendon to see what life is like if you become a cadet.

You can become one, she discovered, if you're a boy or girl aged between sixteen and eighteen. All the training is at Peel Centre in Hendon, where you live in and carry on doing 'O' and 'A' levels. At the same time you do subjects that might be useful in police work, such as sociology, world affairs, liberal studies and law. And, of course, you learn about the practical side of police work; for instance how to cope in situations like accidents and break-ins. Part of each day is devoted to physical training, judo and other arts of self-defence. Then there is the 'adventure playground' which Jenny thought was more like an assault course.

The day had started with a parade at 8.30, and when Jenny left the cadets to go to their various hobbies and evening activities, she felt pretty exhausted but convinced that the cadets were enjoying themselves and were going to have useful careers.

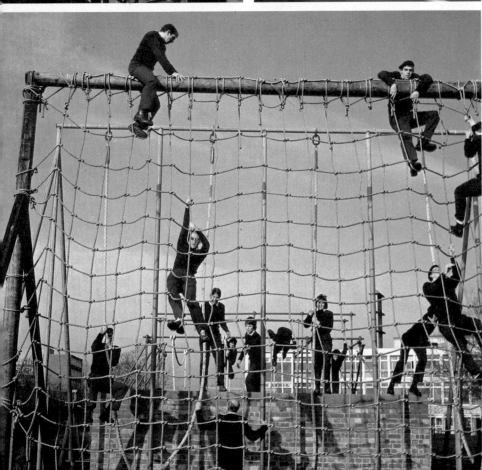

Make & Do Quickies

SHELVES
FILL EMPTY DRINKS CANS WITH SAND OR SOIL TO WEIGHT THEM AND TAPE THEM TOGETHER. USE PAINTED CHIPBOARD FOR THE SHELVES.

LOW TABLE
PAINT TWO BREEZE BLOCKS WITH EMULSION AND USE CHIPBOARD OR ANY OTHER

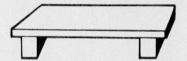

WOOD FOR THE TABLE TOP.

STORAGE CANS

CAREFULLY REMOVE THE LIDS FROM TIN CANS AND REMOVE THEIR LABELS BY SOAKING THEM IN WATER. DECORATE AS YOU LIKE AND USE THEM TO STORE PENCILS, BRUSHES ETC. THEY CAN ALSO BE USED AS BOOKENDS.

PATCHWORK CUSHION
TAKE SIXTEEN 7" SQUARES OF DIFFERENT MATERIAL AND SEW THESE TOGETHER AT THE EDGES TO MAKE UP ONE PIECE 2' SQUARE. JOIN THIS ON THREE SIDES TO A 2' SQUARE PIECE OF MATERIAL AND THEN TURN THE BAG INSIDE OUT. FILL

WITH LOTS OF SCRAPS OF OLD MATERIAL AND OLD TIGHTS, AND THEN NEATLY SEW UP THE FOURTH SIDE.

STORAGE CHESTS

FIND SOME OLD TEA CHESTS (YOU CAN BUY THEM CHEAPLY FROM WAREHOUSES) AND REMOVE ANY NAILS, SHARP BITS OF TIN ETC. SAND-PAPER THE EDGES. PAINT AS YOU LIKE OR STICK PICTURES ON THEM. (USE MASKING TAPE TO HELP YOU GET STRAIGHT LINES IF YOU ARE PAINTING STRIPES.) STAND THE CHESTS ANY WAY YOU LIKE, IN A ROW OR PILED ON TOP OF ONE ANOTHER.

An Ancient Briton Dish : Bowman's Breakfast
Mix together 2 teaspoons of rolled oats and a small peeled and grated apple. Then add 2 teaspoons of currants (or fresh berries), a tablespoon of chopped nuts, 2 teaspoons of honey, and just enough milk to moisten the mixture. Delicious !

A MAZE OF DREAMS

A report on last year's Magpie Annual Competition

The judge of last year's competition, for which you had to send in your plans for the ideal adventure playground, was John Birtwhistle *who wrote the article about playgrounds. Here is his report on the competition.*

I had told a lot of children round where I live that any day now the postman would be bringing a box of all your entries to the Adventure Playground Competition. When it arrived at last, I met them all after school and we had a big meeting to look at every single drawing. A noisy and excited meeting it was too, with everybody pointing out a different thing to everybody else. One of you had named part of her playground *A Maze of Dreams,* and I thought this was a good title for the whole competition.

We ended up by sticking about forty of the best drawings round the walls, and hearing everyone's comments in turn. That gave a pretty good idea of who the winners ought to be. But it was still very hard to sort out definite names, so I also named as many runners-up as possible.

In your playgrounds you seem to be planning a whole world complete in itself. A world with its own builders and farmers, families and armies, shops and fund-raising; its own zoos and governments, newspapers and libraries, graves (for budgies) . . . and, above all, with its own arts and crafts and ways of having fun.

The playground is for everybody in it to enjoy. Whatever is forbidden in the world outside can happen in some way within the playground – whether it is jumping on beds, or getting covered in mud. When one of you designed a 'goal post without netting, to swing from', I imagined him getting ticked off for swinging on the post at school.

Your playgrounds are crammed with things to do, from the 'secret crow's nest' at the top, down to the 'underground art room'. And many of the things can be used in more than one way, like the crab apples which are there for throwing as well as eating. There are a hundred ways of climbing, swinging, rocking, jumping and balancing. Hundreds of ideas about how to get along on wheels, eat, make things (useful or crazy), race, get dirty, run risks, be quiet, let off steam, and entertain oneself and others. Hundreds of types of towers, houses, forts and vehicles.

Hundreds of curious and dramatic objects, like the five-year-old boy's 'Old Fire Engine'. I like 'The Tortoise Tube', 'The Balloon Pit', 'The Mini-Hara Desert' ('Complete with collapsable mirages'), and 'The Race of Different Things'. One would certainly need the 'wooden hut where you can sit when you're so exhausted you can't do anything else'.

Different people like different things, as a lot of you showed in your playgrounds. And the same goes for judging your drawings. I can only say what I thought myself. It seemed to me that the best plans were those that could be used in many different ways – and not, for example, an army obstacle course where you could only go round one set of things in the same order. I was looking for plans which had imagined what the place would be like in all sorts of moods, in all sorts of weathers, and for all sorts and ages of people.

As well as that, the winners not only had good ideas, but also managed to tell you about the feeling of them. As you looked at the drawing, you could tell a bit what it would be like to play in the real place. Children who live in the country very often find their own playgrounds in woods and streams and hills. I suppose what are called 'Adventure Playgrounds' were started by adults who wanted to give town children the same kind of play as in the country. With your drawings, you have accepted some of these adult ideas. You have said No to some. You have changed some. And you have added some of your own. In fact, the ones you have added would make a long list, and I very much hope that they will get built in real playgrounds.

Several of you wrote complaining that you had no reasonable place to play, and wanting some sort of adventure playground. 'There is a place to build it, but it only has blackberries on it'. One of you said, 'I hope when I'm grown up I can organise a playground for children like me who get fed up not having any brothers and sisters and whose friends live far away. I'm always fed up.'

There may be a lot you can do before you are grown up. Try getting together with your friends and pressing adults to give you what you need. One of you wrote about how their playground would be best in a small wood, and if anybody didn't have a wood, 'they could easily get some friends together and go and look for one'.

Winners

Over 10 age-group
Robin Evans (11) of Rossendale, Lancashire
Sandra Brinksman (11) of Warrington, Cheshire

10 and under age-group
Karen Winship (9) of Abranhill, Cumbernauld
Simon Underhill (5) of Birtly, Tyne & Wear

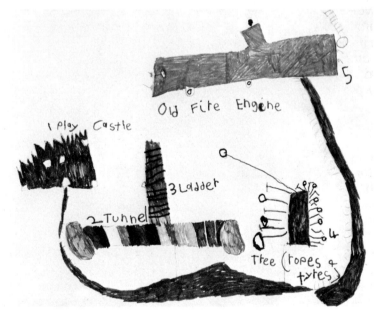

Runners-up
Adrienne Carruthers
Sarah Wilson
Denise Taylor
Elizabeth Rachel Holland
Robert St. Ledger
Paula Devine
Sheelagh O'Sullivan
Karen Watling
Tracy-Jane Barnes

Maddocks

DON'T FORGET WE ARE A NEUTRAL COUNTRY!

NEXT TIME YOU FORGET HIM—
TIE A KNOT IN YOUR HANKY

I THINK WE'VE JUST SEEN THE
FIRST CUCKOO OF THE YEAR!

—YOU MEAN THIS KIND OF LOLLY?

Crack the Code

The poem below is written in code. We would like you to crack the code and read the poem. Then write the title of the poem and the name of its author on a *postcard*, together with your own name and address, and send the postcard to:

GOJAGOJIRBR CP AJARQRL PICB TJKMZAM CELJI
ICSJAN LCBR MC LZQRA JA KOAAW EZDRKMJAR,
SJML Z VZINC CP JQCIW,
ZAT ZERK ZAT ERZVCVFK,
KZATZDSCCT, VRTZISCCT, ZAT KSRRM SLJMR SJAR.

KMZMRDW KEZAJKL NZDDRCA VCBJAN PICB MLR JKMLBOK,
TJEEJAN MLICONL MLR MICEJVK XW MLR EZDB-NIRRA KLCIRK,
SJML Z VZINC CP TJZBCATK,
RBRIZDTK, ZBRMLWKMK,
MCEZYRK, ZAT VJAAZBCA, ZAT NCDT BCJTCIRK.

TJIMW XIJMJKL VCZKMRI SJML Z KZDM-VZFRT KBCFR KMZVF
XOMMJAN MLICONL MLR VLZAARD JA MLR BZT BZIVL TZWK,
SJML Z VZINC CP MWAR VCZD,
ICZT-IZJD, EJN-DRZT,
PJIRSCCT, JICA-SZIR, ZAT VLRZE MJA MIZWK.

Code Competition,
Magpie,
Thames Television,
Teddington Lock,
Middlesex.

The first twenty-five correct answers that are picked out of a hat on 1 February 1977 will win £1 book tokens.

For last year's code, as for this year's, you not only had to crack the code: you also had to give the title and author of the coded poem. Hundreds and hundreds of you proved that you were up to the double task by sending postcards bearing the words 'The Eagle' by Alfred Lord Tennyson.
Congratulations to everyone who sent in correct solutions, and especially to the twenty-five whose cards were the first to be picked out of a hat and who won £1 book tokens:
Catherine Abbott, Richard Baldock, Annette Birchall, Vanessa Brunt, Margaret Burrows, Sarah-Anne Carden, David Curtin, R. Everett, Tina Farrington, Caron Flook, Andrew Hamilton, Avril Haydock, Robert Little, Joe Melvin, Elisabeth Nicolls, Robert Noble, Jean Oliver, Andrea Paxon, Tui Sadler, Anne Scarisbrick, Michael Selwood, Tracie Shaw, Katherine Stevens, Carol Strainge, Ian White.

BOOK SPOT

Jason by J. M. Marks (*Oxford University Press, 40p*)
James is flying back to school from Hong Kong when his plane is hi-jacked. It lands on the outskirts of a jungle and James gets thoroughly involved in all sorts of exciting adventures.

Polar by Elaine Moss, illustrated by Jeanie Baker (*Andre Deutsch, £2.25*)
The delightful adventures of a bear called Polar.

Old Possum's Book of Practical Cats by T.S. Eliot (*Faber, 75p*)
First published in 1939, this paperback edition has colour illustrations. Classic poems about cats of all kinds, including Jellicle cats, the old Gumbie cat, not to mention Growltiger, Mr Mistoffelees, Mungojerrie, Rumpelteazer, and Macavity the Mystery Cat.

Tennis Tips

During the past year David Potter and his pupil Clare Harrison have presented a series of coaching items on Magpie. David is a tennis professional at Sutton Tennis and Squash Club and Clare is National Under-Sixteen Champion of Great Britain. This year, Magpie is following Clare's progress in her first year as one of Britain's youngest and most promising full-time professionals.

Here are a few of David's most important tennis tips.

The best way of getting started, once you've had a bit of fun knocking a ball up against a wall or garage door, is to join a local tennis club. Watch the better players and see how they go about it.

You can learn a lot if you get a job as a ball-boy or ball-girl at a local tournament.

If you decide you would really like to play well, persuade your parents to let you have just one lesson with a professional. He will tell you if you have the ability to become a good player with further training.

The four main strokes of tennis are forehand drive, backhand drive, service and volley.

When you are waiting to play a forehand or backhand drive—when, for example, about to receive service—stand with your feet a little wider apart than your shoulder width, so that you can shift your weight from one foot to the other. Your toes should be pointing at the net.

Hold your racket up, using a grip as though you are shaking hands with the racket. Your other hand should be supporting the racket just under the head. Keep your eyes looking just over the top of the racket, which should be pointing at your opponent. Be very alert.

If the ball comes to your forehand, get into a sideways position, swing the racket back in plenty of time, and strike the ball opposite your left foot which should be forward. Follow through, with all the power coming from your shoulder. At the finish of your swing, the racket should be pointing at the spot where you aimed the ball and you should be balanced.

Most of these points also apply to the backhand. For this stroke you should get even more sideways to the ball, with your right foot forward. The two main differences from the forehand are that you should move your grip to the top of the racket handle, and keep your left hand supporting the swing much longer.

The service, the stroke with which you put the ball into play, is the most important stroke and one that you can practise on your own. Stand just behind the baseline, sideways to the net. Swing your arms slowly apart until you are in a 'hands up' position. At this point the ball should be tossed up from your left hand, high enough for you just to be able to reach it. Deliver the stroke with a throwing action—a fast movement—and as you hit the ball your right leg should swing through on to the court, leaving your left foot balanced in its original position. The racket should finish on the left side of your body.

The volley is the stroke with which you strike the ball before it bounces. It is played with no backswing. You get sideways to the net and punch the racket into the ball as far in front of you as you can reach. Keep the racket head up, and if the ball is low, bend your knees so that your eye level is behind the ball.

All these hints are for right-handed players.
Always watch the ball, especially when your opponent is striking it. Move in small steps when you are near the ball, and practise one thing at a time. You will get worse before you get better.

Both Doug and Mick worked at these tips on the court with David. They both improved very quickly, and you could, too. If you have any queries on tennis, write to David Potter care of Magpie at Teddington, enclosing a stamped, addressed envelope, and he'll be pleased to help you.

Medieval Cooking

In the days of twentieth-century supermarkets and deep freezers which mean that we can get almost any type of food whenever we want it, it's hard to imagine the food situation in medieval times when no one had a refrigerator and the country's few shops stocked a very small range of food-stuffs compared with today.

Poor people had to be content with a largely vegetarian diet, eating onions, kale, dried beans and peas, with lots of bread made with bran. They might eat meat on feast days or if, on pain of death, they managed to poach an animal.

Averagely well-off people had a more varied diet. Meat was generally scarce in those days, but when they could get it, they ate most sorts of meat that we eat today, including some that we don't—crane, for instance, and peacock and swan. Geese and chickens provided popular food, although medieval chickens were much smaller than ours today—about the size of partridges which themselves were a delicacy (Edward I's children ate a partridge each at one medieval feast). Venison was quite a popular sort of meat too. Because meat was scarce, practically every bit of an animal was eaten, including pigs' heads and trotters and calves' feet.

Fish formed an important part of the medieval diet, partly because it was more available than meat and partly because the church dictated that a large number of days had to be meatless —every Friday, for instance, the whole of Lent and some Wednesdays and Saturdays as well. Fish was salted or smoked to preserve it all the year around and large quantities of herrings were kept in this way. Some rich people bred fish in ponds. Carp and pike were especial delicacies, a 3-foot pike costing as much as two pigs. Whale and sturgeon were designated Royal Fish and had to be sent to the King if caught. Many people cultivated eels in ditches, because eels taste a bit like meat, in fact meat pies were often served with a green sauce made from the liquor of stewed eels. A schoolboy of the times remarked, 'They will not believe how weary I am of fish, and how much I desire that flesh were come in again.' In return for being allowed to use a tract of land near Norwich, those townsfolk had to give the King 24 fresh-herring pies, each pie containing at least five herrings and flavoured with ginger, pepper, cinnamon and other spices.

The use of spices had been introduced by Crusaders returning from the East. They also brought back sugar, brown rice, dried fruits such as sultanas, almonds and oranges, none of which had been eaten before in England.

and beans were eaten, as were plenty of onions, leeks and semi-wild root vegetables.

Lots of eggs were used, but just as the chickens were very small, so were their eggs, and people bought them by the hundred. One Easter, the Countess of Warwick bought 3,700 eggs for just 52 pence!

Piemakers did good business, selling both savoury pies and sweet ones, including 'flawn' (a kind of custard flan), cheesecakes and wafer biscuits. And bakers sold standard-sized white loaves (called 'wastels') for a farthing each.

In medieval times, fireplaces were moved from the centre of the kitchen to an outside wall so that smoke could escape without contaminating the room. Ovens for baking were built at one side of the fire, but most cooking was done in front of the fire on a spit or in a cauldron hanging from inside the chimney.

The cauldron was a very useful container and whole dinners were often cooked inside it, each item of food appropriately enclosed. In a typical cauldron, for instance, you might find wrapped bacon, a jar of beef and birch twigs (to make a kind of beef tea), a jar of pork and poultry and onions, all pressed down with stones, a linen bag of cereals and a bag of beans.

When Mick, Douglas and Jenny told you about medieval cooking on the programme, they finished up by eating a typical medieval meal. The first course was chicken cooked on a spit and basted with honey. Then came a choice of stewed eels or herring pie. Pigs' trotters in parsley sauce were the next delicacy, followed by marchpane and apple tansy. And the whole lot was washed down with ale.

The two puddings were very easy to make, as Mick and Doug discovered, so here are the recipes.

Medieval people didn't eat vegetables with meat; instead they were eaten as a separate dish. Carrots and cauliflowers were not yet known, but peas

Marchpane

Ingredients
6 oz icing sugar
4 oz ground almonds
$\frac{1}{2}$ teaspoon almond essence
1 large egg (separated)
few drops lemon juice
few glacé cherries

Method
Sieve the icing sugar into a bowl, stir in the ground almonds and add the almond essence, egg yolk and a few drops of lemon juice (just enough to bind the ingredients into a pliable paste). Knead until smooth. Onto a board lightly sprinkled with cornflour, roll the mixture to a square shape about $\frac{1}{2}''$ thick. Transfer to a non-stick baking sheet or a baking sheet lined with greaseproof paper. Using the back of a knife, mark out diamond shapes and press a quarter of a glacé cherry into each diamond. Lightly beat the egg white, and brush it over the marchpane. Bake in a hot oven (425/Mk 7) for a few minutes until the surface is nicely browned. Remove the baking sheet from the oven, leave until cool, and cut into diamonds.

Apple tansy

Ingredients
2 medium cooking apples
1 oz butter
1 large egg
½ pint milk
2 level tablespoons soft brown sugar
¼ teaspoon mixed spice
4 oz white breadcrumbs

Method
Peel and core the apples and cut them into slices.
Cook very gently in the butter until soft. Break
the egg into a basin, whisk in the milk, add the
sugar and mixed spice. Tip in the breadcrumbs and
apple and stir thoroughly. Turn into a 1½ to 2 pint
greased ovenproof dish and bake in a preheated
oven (325/Mk 3) until set (about 30 minutes).
Serve with bramble or redcurrant jelly on top.

Cartoon Competition

For this year's *Annual* competition we thought it would be fun if we asked you to draw a cartoon. The obvious person to consult about the competition was Peter Maddocks who has often drawn cartoons for the *Annual*. So we rang him up and asked him what he thought.

'Great idea,' he said, 'it'll encourage youngsters to draw cartoons instead of wasting their time doing sums.' So would he help judge the competition? 'I'd love to,' he replied, 'I could probably pinch some ideas.'

Then we thought, the competition should have a subject, otherwise how would you know where to begin? 'Tell them that the cartoon must include a bird,' said Peter Maddocks. 'After all, you've got a Murgatroyd bird on the show. There could be a chicken, a vulture, a duck, an ostrich, a magpie or any type of bird just so long as there's a bird.'

So that was it: we'd like you to send us a cartoon with a bird in it.
But what would Peter be looking for when judging the competition? 'Well,' he said, 'I shall be looking for two things: first, the joke must be funny, and secondly, it must be drawn with a sense of fun. A cartoon is something you *look* at, then laugh. So although I shan't be looking for superb craftsmanship in the drawing, I don't want competitors to send in just illustrated jokes. The drawing should be funny as well as the idea. In the end, I'll give prizes to the cartoons that make me laugh most.'
The competition is divided into two age-groups: ten and under, and over ten. The winner in each age-group will appear on the programme to receive their prize. To enter the competition, send your cartoon not later than 31 January 1977 to

Cartoon Competition,
Magpie,
Thames Television,
Teddington Lock,
Middlesex.

Remember to include your name, address and age.

Smithy Quiz Answers
1. 'The Blacksmith'.
2. St Ely.
3. Improver.
4. Journeyman.
5. Handel.
6. Legend has it that Nick the Devil kept tormenting St Ely; so St Ely shod Nick with a red-hot shoe saying he would remove it only if Nick promised never to torment him again. Hopping in agony, Nick agreed and has ever since steered clear of horseshoes.
7. 'The Tiger' by William Blake.

BAM BAM BAM

MADDOCKS.

— HE HATES INDIANS!

MAGPIE TEAM, 1975-6
Tim Jones (*producer*) ; Lesley Burgess (*associate producer*) ; Neville Green, Richard Mervyn, John Russell, Audrey Starrett, Peter Yolland (*directors*) ; Helen Best, Ted Clisby, Martyn Day, Helen Dickinson, Sam Hanson, Kate Marlow, Gillian Trethowan (*researchers*) ; Cherry Crompton, Dorothy Friend, Maggi Hilliard, Pat Maclaurin, Penny Welsford (*production assistants*) ; Terry Harris, Tony O'Toole, John Plummer, David Rush (*film editors*) ; Bernie Cooper, Chris Thompson, John Wright (*assistant film editors*) ; Jean Lyall (*secretary*) ; Marion Howells, Heather Meredith, Marita Samuels, Pat Wise (*correspondence girls*).

MAGPIE ANNUAL 1977
Editor : Alison Wade
Designer : Helen Lindon
Editorial Assistant : Vicki Webster
Magpie Annual 1977 © 1976, Thames Television

ACKNOWLEDGEMENTS
For permission to reproduce illustrations Thames Television would like to thank : Eric Auerbach (*Stomu Yamash'ta*), George Wilkes (*Ace, Flame*), W. Jordan & Sons (*Flour photographs*), Frank Lindon (*Fun-Art Farm*), Gerald Sunderland (*Round London Marathon, Grand Prix, Owzat!*), Pat Elliot Shircore (*House of Glass*), Tate Gallery, London (*Vincent Van Gogh: 'The Chair and the Pipe', Thomas Gainsborough: 'The Market Cart'*), Marwell Zoo (*Endangered Species*), Tom Ravensdale (*Clare Harrison*), Keystone Press Agency (*Chris Evert, Jimmy Connors, Bjorn Borg, Evonne Cawley*), Barnaby's Picture Library (*Arthur Ashe*), Weaver Smith Collection, Thames Television (*Medieval Cooking drawings*), TV Times (*presenters at medieval banquet*). Endpapers by Mick Manville and Pat Elliot Shircore.

SOME OF THE MAGPIE ITEMS THAT YOU CAN BUY
Magpie Numbers Game (*Omnia Pastimes Ltd*) ; an exciting game in which you compete to make sums out of figures and signs.
Magpie Bookends (*Escor Toys Ltd*) ; to prop up all your books.
Magpie Kite (*Condor Toys Ltd*) ; a large Murgatroyd flies on it.
Magpie Jigsaws (*Condor Toys Ltd*) ; a range of four showing Jenny, Mick, Doug and all three in the studio.
Magpie Pocket Books (*Lutterworth Press Ltd*) ; the titles in print are 'Civil Aircraft', 'Horses and Ponies', 'Fish and Fishing', 'Birds of the Countryside', and 'Prehistoric Animals'.
'A Diary of Yesterdays' (*Piccolo Books*) ; written by Tony Bastable, there's an interesting entry for each day of the year.

Published in Great Britain by World Distributors (Manchester) Ltd, 12 Lever Street, Manchester M60 1TS

SBN 7235 0395 8

Printed and bound by Jarrolds of Norwich